# Hope Elevated

How to accept your past, gain clarity, and develop a healthy mindset

Tamar Medford

## Disclaimer:

The events and conversations in this book have been set down to the best of the author's ability, although some names and details have been changed to protect the privacy of individuals.

## Content Warning:

This book contains some adult material and language including stories about or referencing physical assault, drug and alcohol abuse, suicidal thoughts, as well as depression.

**Hope Elevated:** How to accept your past, gain clarity, and develop a healthy mindset



ISBN 978-1-7772556-0-2

July, 2020

For more information, visit www.theroadforward.ca

## DEDICATION

This book is dedicated to all those people who want to empower themselves and create a firm belief in their own abilities to change their lives.

## SPECIAL THANKS

To my mother and father, who raised me to become the person I am today as well as my best friend, Beverly, who has been my rock through it all. To Gene, my spouse, for being there when I need you, supporting me through this process, and always keeping my life fun. To my friends who stuck by my side through addiction even when it was hard to watch. Thank you for believing in me and following me into my world of recovery. You helped me realize that I could be a better human being. To all the people who came into my life at the time I recovered or beyond. You continue to help me grow and encouraged me to believe that I am capable of so much more. I couldn't have done this without you all, and I want you to know just how grateful I am that you are part of my journey.

Thank you to everyone who has purchased this book. Without you, I would not have been inspired to write this and spread a message of hope.

## TESTIMONIALS

Tamar's journey is incredibly captivating from the very first chapter and inspires you to follow along right through to the end! Her stories are engaging, and she shares in a relatable way. Tamar experiences some powerful lessons from her struggles with addiction that allows the reader to implement into their own lives as well. I highly encourage you to read this astonishing book. A must-read! **- Paula Miller, Lost AF Wellness**

**IG:** @paula4miller
**Podcast:** Lost AF Wellness

Tamar's steady and incredible growth comes with valuable qualities, of which I have been blessed to reap the benefits. Her story of overcoming addiction is one of internal strength, faith, hope, and dedication to change. She has a remarkable life story and has overcome adversity through healthy life habits, discipline, and consistency. As a result, Tamar is now a coach who applies her own experiences to instill success in others. Her solid and steady coaching style is a capsule of knowledge, love, and patience. As my coach, I highly recommend her coaching services and this incredible book. Pick up a copy of HOPE ELEVATED, and it will do precisely that. **- Flossie Njama, Simple Life Healthier You**

**Facebook:** Simple Life Healthier U Family
**Website:** www.simplelifehealthieryou.com

In all of our lives, we have dark moments, times we've bottomed-out, or perhaps we are in the midst of one of these places right now. People often take two paths. The first is to block the past from our minds and push ahead. That never works because our history is always with us. The second is that they get stuck in the past and make it their eternal present, and it keeps holding them back in the same pain and patterns that took them down in the first place. In this book, Tamar Medford shares so honestly, so openly and so clearly how she found a path out of the shame, judgment, and manipulation that was keeping her where she was – stuck in the patterns that kept her at her bottom. Through honesty with herself, self-empowerment, and creating the path to making better choices, Tamar unlocked not only a different road for herself but the inspiration for each of us to do the same. **- Bryan Falchuk, CPT BCS, Best-Selling Author, & Speaker**

**Website:** bryanfalchuk.com
**Podcast:** Do a Day with Bryan Falchuk

We've all had painful moments in our past we're not exactly proud of, and for a while, we can convince ourselves that boxing that pain up and shoving it in the back of the closet means that we've 'moved on.' In the meantime, that pain is festering and poisoning our present life, and we're left wondering why we're stuck in the same patterns that made us miserable in the first place. Tamar has courageously taken that box out of the closet and faced her pain without shaming, blaming, or judging herself. Her honesty is refreshing and endearing, as she bravely revisits her journey with accountability and self-forgiveness that is truly inspiring. A great read! **- Jennifer Knapp, Founder of Shameless Solutions, Inc.**

**Website:** www.shamelesssolutions.com

## READER BONUS

Check out The Road to Health Website to access the reader bonus content!

Wake Up on Fire Workshop (FREE) www.theroadforward.ca

* Recommended Reading

* Atomic Habits - James Clear
* Food Heals - Allison Melody
* Sleep Smarter - Shawn Stevenson
* Meant for More - Lisa Sasevich
* Any many more!

Find it all at: www.theroadforward.ca

Don't forget to check out the Tips & Resources section in the back of the book to get a list of my favourite podcasts as well as some other resources I have used in my journey!

## FOREWORD

One of my favorite things to tell my coaching clients is that I realize that they aren't in a space of positive momentum right now, but the good news is that they can borrow some of my positive mojo until they build up their own. This simple step can ignite that first spark of HOPE that they actually can reclaim control over their life and their health. I remember having a similar conversation with Tamar back when I first started coaching her, and now she is ready to offer you the same deal.

When I did my first coaching session with Tamar, I asked her to do two very important things:

#1. Accept personal responsibility for where her life currently stood: the good, bad, and ugly.

#2. Be willing to give up control of the game planning portion of her health journey to me so that we can get her going in the right direction again.

Being the uber coachable person that Tamar is, she crushed it with both of these difficult starting points and quickly became one of my best clients and now a team member with my community that I trust to mentor and lead.

Tamar's life experiences and her willingness to be completely open, honest, and vulnerable with you is a true gift that you will receive by reading this book. She speaks from the heart, and she's trying to help you avoid a few of the life pitfalls that she's experienced, and she gives you a road map to escape them......just in case you are in the thick of it.

Momentum is a precious commodity, and it is often misunderstood. Many people think that they can flip a magic switch and proclaim, "Now I am in POSITIVE MOMENTUM with my entire life!".....sorry my friends.....it doesn't quite work that way! I view our life momentum like a highway. There are roads that take you in the correct direction (positive momentum), roads that take you in the wrong direction (negative momentum), and on/off ramps that help you change direction.

I want you to view this book and all the coaching that Tamar has put together for you as your off-ramp from the road of negative momentum. You will be able to absorb the life lessons and then implement to the best of your ability to reclaim control over your life and ignite some incredible positive momentum.

Remember this: Reclaiming control over your health and

your life might very well be the hardest thing that you ever do……but the good news is that YOU ARE WORTH THE EFFORT!

Adam Schaeuble….aka…The PHD (previously heavy dude)
Host of the top-ranked health podcast The Million Pound Mission.

# INTRODUCTION

Hey everyone, my name is Tamar Medford, and I'm glad you could join me for this adventure. Hope Elevated takes you through my journey of addiction and into the world after recovery and beyond. I am a professional life coach, host of The Road to Health Podcast, as well as a champion for people who suffer from addiction.

The reason I wrote this book was for anyone out there that is struggling to empower themselves to develop a firm belief in their own ability to change their lives. Why, might you ask? Well, because at several points in my life, I created the belief system that I was not good enough, that I wouldn't amount to anything and also that I was incapable of becoming a better person. If you can relate and have felt this way before, I want to tell you, you ARE capable of so much more than you can even imagine. I've come to realize that our experiences, no matter how bad, can be a gift with which we can use to share hope with others who struggle as well. It can also empower us to do things we never thought were possible. In this book, I will get vulnerable and share stories about my life that I'm not proud of. However, I now believe that to create change in our lives, we need to accept our past as it was and move forward. I have never entirely shut the door because it serves as a reminder of what I do not want to return to. My past inspires me to continue to move forward, work on myself, and help others to do the same. It shows me how far I've come and also gives me the belief of how much more I'm capable of. I also believe the same for you, so I hope you enjoy this book as much as I enjoyed writing it, even though it was scary as hell.

I grew up having a fantastic childhood, and so when I drank for the first time, I thought my behaviors mirrored an average person. I had always assumed that to be classified as an addict/alcoholic, you had to have specific qualifications or hit bottom to the degree where you had nothing left. Well, my friends, I have since come to the understanding that this is far from the truth. Addiction is a disease where I react differently to substances than one without dependency would experience. When I first sobered up, I would question whether or not I was actually an alcoholic. I had heard stories of others who suffered from addiction, and their bottoms just seemed so much worse. Then someone in my early sobriety told me, "You hit your bottom when you decide to stop digging." This statement was one I could understand, and it opened my eyes. I think we all experience or hit bottoms in our lives, and we can let that inspire us to move forward, or as I have many times in the past, let it drag us down further. Regardless, my bottom had nothing to do with what classified me as being an alcoholic, it was how my body responded to that first drink. Today I realize that there are many things I turn to for ease and comfort aside from drugs and alcohol. Whenever I feel an emotion that seems too big to cope with, I turn to my favorite food. When I have a stressful day at work, or I'm stuck in traffic, it's easier to reach for fast food than it is to let myself have a good cry. Through the years and with the help of many incredible people in my life, I have learned how to lessen using food or other things to obtain that instant gratification I often seek. I find I can now sit in my feelings and just allow them to pass. I do this by confiding in others and not being ashamed of what I feel.

Throughout my journey, I ended up in places I honestly thought I was too good for. The power of addiction made it almost impossible to avoid. I hear a lot of people say that we as addicts have a choice, and it's not a topic I'm going to get into right now, but I can tell you from a lot of experience that when I have that first drink my power of choice vanishes. I go from being a shy, insecure girl to someone who has no regard for the feelings of others. I would have moments of clarity along the way, but those moments were always short-lived. I only cared about myself and how I was going to get my next fix. I'm grateful that I was one of the lucky people who made it out alive because I know many people personally who have not. It breaks my heart that some of those people will never get to experience what I have. There are many instances where I wanted to give up on life because I felt as though I would just continue to harm people who were important to me if I just stuck around. I have a lot of compassion for people today who find themselves in this same position because I know what it feels like to be hopeless. I am incredibly grateful that by the right people entering my life at the right time, I was able to start to build a life worth living.

When I got sober in 2012, my protective shield called alcohol had been removed. It felt as though I went back to being that insecure little 14-year-old girl again. Emotions I had never felt came flooding in, and the dams opened up. I cried more in that first year than I think I have in my entire life. Alcohol and drugs had always been my solution. It allowed me to suppress my emotions and feelings so I could stay numb to everything. I never invested in other means to handle what life threw at me. I felt as though the one thing that had always protected me in good times and in bad was gone. I had to learn how to live life again, and that wasn't easy. I learned what it was like to move through fear and experience rejection. I developed faith in something greater than myself to help guide me through situations I hadn't experienced before. This also helped me see that all my needs would always be met no matter what I faced.

Many of the events in this book are memories that stood out to me. They are written to the best of my knowledge as I remember them. I spent a lot of my time in blackouts, so some events are a little fuzzy. As I wrote the book, many memories came up through the process that I have long since hidden away. I was ashamed of the person I was during those times and also how I hurt many people I loved. By sharing this part of my life with you, it has allowed me to begin to heal parts of my life, I didn't even realize needed healing. This story is about my journey through addiction, obesity, and low self-esteem. I share how I found recovery and how I have built the life I have today.

I hope you enjoy walking alongside me throughout this journey and hearing the lessons I learned along the way. I have added a section at the end of every chapter where there are questions that you can feel free to answer and even email me about if you would like some feedback. These can be used as a means of personal exploration and can lead to growth in your own life. I have found that when I write out my story and experiences, I can often see the roadblocks that have stood in my way of becoming who I am truly meant to be. When you write your answers, go back over them and see if you can identify your own patterns or behaviors that you may want to change or adjust. This process is the start of something truly incredible. It allows us to be aware of our patterns and re-write a better story for our future. Enjoy!

If you have any questions along the way feel free to contact me at info@theroadtohealth.me

## THE EARLY YEARS

To start my story off, I thought I would give you a look into my childhood. Some people believe that addicts are created based on terrible traumatic upbringings or unfortunate circumstances that one has had to endure through childhood. Although sadly, this is often the case, and many people who suffer from addiction have a story like this to share, it's not the truth for everyone. I used to think the same way before I finally came to the acceptance that I was an alcoholic myself and learned to understand why. I also had the belief that just because I drank more than the average person but had a good upbringing, I couldn't possibly fit the stereotype of an alcoholic or a drug addict. I thought I was too good for that life, and so I considered myself a heavy drinker and looked at my life as a relatively normal one. What I've learned from my experience over the last 40 plus years, is what makes me an alcoholic is the way I react to a drink when it enters my system. Most people have a few drinks, get a bit of a buzz and realize it's time to stop, and on the rare occasion, they may tie one on and then suffer the consequences of a hangover after which makes them stop. Well, that's not me, folks! I have a whole other reaction to alcohol, and it rarely ends well. For that reason, I wanted to mention before we jump in, that I have changed some names referenced in this book to protect the privacy of specific individuals. I hope you enjoy this book and that by sharing my story, I can bring you some hope that no matter what you've gone through or are going through, there is hope to create a better life.

I was born in The Netherlands on February 11th, 1976. My parents immigrated to Canada when I was only a year old. They wanted a better life for us, and my Dad bought a bakery in a town called Hinton, AB. Now, if you've ever been to Hinton, Alberta, or have heard of it, you are probably wondering, WTF! And trust me, now that I look back, I kind of wonder the same thing. It was an opportunity for them regardless, so off we went. I don't remember the first few years of my life, but when I was three, my little brother was born. I remember having a wonderful childhood, and mostly my brother and I got along well. There was the occasion that he pissed me off by driving his toy car into my well designed and built Lego house, but when that happened, I used to yell at him and repeat the Dutch swear words I had heard my parents use. They weren't too happy about this, and neither was my brother. The only time I had really gotten in trouble those first four years was when my mom got called into my preschool. Apparently, I wouldn't shut up, so the teacher was concerned about my behavior and not impressed. For those of you that know me now, you know I'm still somewhat disruptive, but I own that shit!

During our time in Alberta, we had family from Holland occasionally come over and visit for a few weeks at a time. I remember these visits fondly. I remember my Aunt coming over to stay with us for a year around the time my brother was born, and my grandparents came over often. We went back to Holland a few times here and there when I was young, but I don't remember the details of these trips, just that it was hard to come home and not have that extended family to be around. I loved having a Dad that was a baker because it allowed us to go visit the bakery after school and eat free donuts. My first experience observing addiction was one of these afternoons as we hung out at the bakery. A woman who was well known in the town we lived in was high on something and locked herself in the bathroom. The police showed up and dragged her off, and I just remember thinking, "Why would anyone want to act that way?" but again, I was too young to understand what addiction could do to someone, and to all of us, she just seemed like a crazy person. But mostly I remember enjoying those younger years, other than watching the movie Jaws and Poltergeist way too young. These two movies have scarred me for life, and today I still can't watch horror movies or swim in a body of water where I can't see the bottom.

My Dad enjoyed baking, but his genuine passion was film making. He had grown up having that as his hobby and took on some extra work around town to film documentaries because it was what he enjoyed doing. A few years in, he made his dream come true and started a new film business. Hinton, Alberta wasn't exactly bursting with film opportunities, so our parents decided we would move to British Columbia. My Dad figured that being close to Vancouver would benefit the business, and there would be more work out this way. I enjoyed the first few years of living out in BC because we lived in an area with a vast forest and spent a lot of time outdoors with our friends. It also didn't smell as bad as Hinton did, so that was a bonus.

I have memories of riding my bike for what seemed like miles down to the 7-Eleven to grab a Slurpee and then putting ourselves through the torture of the brain freeze time and time again. This is also the time in my life where I had my first experience with religion. I didn't grow up going to church, but our friends across the street would often invite us on a Sunday so my parents could be alone. My brother and I enjoyed it a lot because it was mostly fun, other than the service itself, which back then we didn't understand all that much. As we learned more about God and religion, we took this information home to our parents. In our house, we didn't look at right or wrong to determine where we ended up when we died, so my parents didn't enjoy hearing us tell them they had to stop drinking wine, or they would end up in hell. This is the first time I had felt any tension concerning religion. My parents would tell us things were ok, and the church would tell us otherwise. Looking back today, I just really didn't understand what it meant to have faith in God or a higher power. I really enjoyed going to church back then because I felt as though they always had so much fun and everyone was so friendly. I had even gone up on stage during one service to be saved, and when I came home all excited and told my parents that I was now going to heaven, I don't think they were all that impressed, or at least not as excited as I was.

The first time I kissed a boy was when I was about 9 years old. This wasn't something that I had planned on doing or something I really knew anything about. We had our babysitter over for the evening, and she was about 7 years older than we were. She had two younger brothers who we were friends with, so when my parents went away, all three of them would come over for the evening, which was a lot of fun. One of those evenings, we were hanging out when our babysitter suggested we play a game called truth or dare. We all agreed because we did not understand what the game was about, but it sounded like fun. At first, she started us off with some innocent dares and truths, which had us laughing a lot. After a few rounds, our sitter looked over at me and said, "Tamar, truth or dare?" I didn't have a lot of secrets to share, and so far, everything seemed harmless and fun, so I went with a dare. She smiled at me and said, "Ok, I want you to French Kiss my older brother for at least 10 seconds." My first question was, "What is a French Kiss?" I wasn't sure about this dare because first, I wasn't at the age where I even knew there were unique styles of kissing options available. Second, other than the crush I had on a boy from school who I traded hockey cards with on break just to be around, I had never kissed a boy. She explained how to do it, and off I went. To be honest, it wasn't an experience I enjoyed at all. The rest of the dares that followed involved a little more kissing and some light touching that I thought was wrong, but I played along. None of this felt right back then, but it sure would discourage me from wanting to kiss a boy again anytime soon!

I never really had to deal with much grief as a child, and I consider myself very fortunate for that. I think the most traumatic thing that happened to me as a kid was when one of our family friends came to visit from Alberta. My friend Adam and I were outside hanging out with our brothers when he went to go lay down beside the trampoline. I asked him what was wrong, and he just said he wasn't feeling well. We hung out and watched movies for the rest of the night, but it wasn't the same Adam I knew back when we lived in Hinton. Regardless, the visit was enjoyable, and we loved staying connected. Although I don't remember the exact time frame, I believe it was a few months later we received a call from Adam's parents letting us know that he was in the hospital and sick with leukemia. Now for a 12-year-old, it didn't make much sense. We had just seen him, and although he wasn't feeling well, it didn't look like he had an illness that could kill him. Unfortunately, a short time later, Adam passed and at such a young age. I remember being so sad for a time but it was hard to understand loss. Years later, we received a visit from the family, and when Adam's youngest brother walked into our home, it was shocking how identical they looked. His youngest brother was only about 1 or 2 when Adam passed, so it was like seeing a ghost.

Not long after that, we ended up moving closer to the city. My Dad was commuting a lot and wanted to be closer to his office. I was sad to be leaving our friends again because we had all grown so close over the last few years and had so many great times, but now we were onto a new adventure. We moved out to Surrey, BC, into a townhome complex. This was the first time we didn't live in a house with a yard, so it was a little strange to be right next to your neighbor. The day we arrived I went for a walk around the complex to go check out my new surroundings. There was a golf course that ran through the middle of the complex, which we thought was pretty cool even though we had never played golf before. We came to a pond just up the road, so my brother and I sat down to watch the ducks swimming around.

A girl came by and sat down next to us. She started throwing breadcrumbs into the pond. When she finished, she looked over and said, "Hi, my name is Julia, are you new here?" I looked over and nodded, and from that day on, Julia and I were inseparable. We would often walk down to the store together and grab cigarettes for her mom and a bag full of one cent candies for ourselves. I know what you're thinking, one cent candies??!!! Yes, this was back in the good old days when you could have a dollar and get enough candy to keep you wired for the entire afternoon. After grabbing our candy and cigarettes, Julia and I went to hang out in a concrete tube that was placed on the side of the golf course. We did not understand why it was there, but it was the perfect spot to hang out and not be seen by anyone! As we opened the bag with all our treats inside, Julia asked me if I had ever tried a cigarette before. I was 12 years old at the time, so I had done little of anything exciting or rebellious. I responded, "No, but I'm kind of curious what it's like." She had asked for a second pack of cigarettes that day, which wasn't the norm, so I couldn't help but wonder if they were for us. She opened the pack and handed me one. As I lit the cigarette and inhaled for the first time, I started coughing. Although the smoke felt harsh on my throat, I loved the buzz I received from it. Julia and I began to laugh because it was fairly obvious she had never smoked before either. Back then, smoking wasn't something that people frowned upon like they do today, well unless you were the parents of a 12-year-old that shouldn't be smoking in the first place. After we finished the first one, we had one more because both of us loved the head rush that came along with it. I wanted to make sure I got enough in before I went home as obviously this wasn't something I had planned on telling my parents about. We thought we were the coolest 12-year-olds in the complex, and we thought smoking made us look badass. I ran home and immediately went to the bathroom to go wash my hands and spray myself down with air freshener. I didn't want to get in trouble with my mom. To this day, I don't think my parents ever knew I smoked because I hid that and a lot of other things reasonably well. I enjoyed the rush of getting away with something I shouldn't be doing, so it became a bit of a game for me.

When the school year started, it wasn't hard to adjust because I had already made friends that summer, which made it easier to fit in. We all hung out together after school, smoking and vandalizing the construction site by our school after the workers would leave for the day. We loved to destroy things and feel the power of getting away with it. One activity that became a common occurrence was playing truth or dare in the trees behind the school. As you know, the first time I was introduced to this game, I was too young to understand it. This time around I really enjoyed it, I mean at 12 who wouldn't want the attention of a boy, right? I also remember being allowed to have my first boy-girl party at this age. We watched the movie Top Gun, and when the sex scene came on, none of us could take our eyes off the screen. If I remember correctly, I think one boy even asked if we could rewind the scene, and so we did. Thank God my parents gave us some privacy back then. I felt very fortunate with the amount of freedom and trust my parents provided me. Those were some fun times in my life and harmless, mostly other than the construction workers we ended up pissing off. When I wasn't hanging out with friends, I was playing soccer. I really enjoyed it because it allowed me to spend some time with my Dad, and I was always looking for his approval, so soccer was one way I got it. My Dad was super involved in my life when I was younger, and I really enjoyed those years and the time I spent with him. He was hard on me because he always expected the best, which improved my skills, and I became a better player because of it. Another reason I enjoyed soccer so much was because it was something I was good at, and I received the validation I was always looking for from my Dad, which made me feel good about myself.

After 6th grade, my parents decided we would move again. We moved to a house in a town called Aldergrove, BC. Even though I hated to leave my friends once again, it was nice to be in a home where we had a backyard. I didn't love the fact that I would have to start over again at a new school and make new friends, but I was grateful that I had one more year to go before I started high school because it meant I had time to make some friends by then. In grade 7, I had my first official boyfriend. I was super excited he had noticed me, and by this time, I felt I had practiced kissing enough, so I was ready to be the perfect girlfriend. He would walk me home from school every day and was adamant that we held hands. I thought it was so sweet and felt like such a grownup. We dated for a whole two weeks before he dumped me for being what he called a freeze. Now, if you've never heard the term freeze used before, it means that apparently, I didn't want to put out. Although he had given me a kiss on the lips a few times, we had never moved past that point. I found it a little strange because I was ready to go should he want to progress further; after all, I had practiced! A few days later, I found out he had dated one of my best friends, and not surprising a couple of weeks after that, he left her for the same reasons he left me. I believe he went through the entire 7th-grade class and never found love that year, unfortunately. I figured once we went to high school, we would meet some more mature guys, so I was looking forward to the change.

The first year of high school wasn't at all what I thought it would be like. I went in assuming that I would be in the same classes as my friends were, but it ended up being the complete opposite. I felt like I was starting over again, and it wasn't a feeling I enjoyed because I had done it a few times now. I wasn't sure exactly where I fit in but made friends with a few groups of people and because I still smoked occasionally; I became friends with some kids that hung out in the smoke hole at lunch so I could always have a cigarette here and there. Some of my other friends, however, hated smoking, so I would play both sides. I signed up for almost every sport I could because it was an excellent way to get to know others I hadn't met yet. It was that age where I just wanted to fit in and feel important. I was very insecure and remembered one afternoon that I was walking home from school when a couple of boys walked by and made fun of me. They said I had a big butt and looked like a boy. I had also recently gotten my hair cut short, which is a whole other story which we won't get into, but needless to say, those comments, followed by laughter, hurt. I had a curvy body for which today I'm proud of, but back then, it crushed me to think two boys I didn't even know could make fun of me for something I couldn't control. After that, I started to worry that maybe all boys thought this way about me, which would eventually lead to the attention I would seek from men to prove that theory wrong. I ran home and examined myself in the bathroom mirror for what felt like hours. Tears streamed down my face as I wondered if maybe the boys were right and I was fat. I was already developing low self-esteem and became super sensitive whenever someone said something negative because I always assumed they were talking about me. I told myself stories that were so far from the truth, but to me, they were real. This was when my people-pleasing skills were also set into motion. So here I was 14 years old, not sure where I belonged and developing that body shame that followed me right into my adult life. I felt as though I was on a mission to prove something to anyone who would notice, and it was exhausting. I was seeking validation in all areas of my life, and even if I received the recognition, it still wasn't good enough, nor did it fill the void I felt inside of me. I needed to find a solution to quiet the voices in my head, and sure enough, a short time later, I would find that solution.

I continued to sign up for various sports, which included volleyball, basketball, soccer, track and field, and even gymnastics. If I could just excel at one of these, maybe people would notice me. Though I did well at most sports, if I wasn't the best, I would usually end up quitting after a time. Gymnastics was one of those sports I was not very good at because I could not even master a simple cartwheel, and I wasn't flexible at all. To be honest, I still cannot do a cartwheel today, and I have tried, but it usually ends up with me pulling a muscle, so I avoid such activities. I had a few friends that had also joined gymnastics, so it was more of a social outing than anything. Here is a fun fact for you, I didn't know it then, but I would meet someone in that class that would later change the course of my life entirely.

I enjoyed being part of the team until the school bully had arrived. I'm not at all sure what she was doing there because she did not enjoy class; I believe they forced her to be there, which didn't benefit the rest of us. She was tall and mean and could intimidate most of us just by the look in her eyes. We did our best to avoid her, but it wasn't always possible. To make matters worse, she would often start arguing with our coach, and one of those afternoons, our coach asked me to please go down to the office and file a report. I was scared out of my mind because there was no way I would report the one person in the school that could beat the shit out of me and had a history of doing so to many others. I wandered the hallway for about 30 minutes and avoided the principal's office at all costs. As I walked back to the gym, I was suddenly grabbed and pinned against a locker. She looked at me with anger in her eyes and said, "Did you report me?" I answered, "No, I swear!"

She eased up on her grip and said, "Good! Trust me, if I find out you did, I will come after you and beat the shit out of you." She let go, and I returned to class. Although this would be my last run-in with her in high school, on a side note about twenty-plus years later, I would run into her while out with some friends for dinner. Ironically, one friend I was with that evening was from that gymnastics class. We all recognized the waitress right away because she was hard to forget. After dinner, we went to pay the bill, and as I entered my pin number, I accidentally hit cancel instead of ok. As I smiled and apologized to the waitress, she laughed and then went all serious and said, "I'll forgive you this time, but if you do it again, I'll beat the shit out of you." I knew she was joking, but all three of us looked at each other and burst out laughing because it wasn't the first time I had heard her say that. It's funny when you run into people from the past, but the circumstances have totally changed.

I learned a lot from those younger years. It didn't matter how many friends I had or if I fit in; I didn't love myself. My parents and others around me showed me so much love, but yet I kept searching for another external solution to make me feel important and whole. I tried to be perfect at everything, and when I wasn't, it just proved my ego right that, in fact, I was not good enough. I grew up developing the belief that I had to be a certain way and follow the crowd rather than be myself and pursue my own passions and dreams. Back then, you graduated, went to university, got married, and had kids. This is the way it was for many people I knew, and because I wasn't achieving any of this in my life, I felt less than. I know people today who struggle with society's view of where you should be in your life by a specific age. I had a great childhood; I made mistakes along the way, but I don't regret the experiences I've been through. I have learned to love myself as a result of accepting my past. I am right where I need to be at this moment, and because of these experiences, I now have a story I can use to help others. I had to learn how to be myself, which meant being vulnerable and real sometimes, no matter how hard it was.

**Lessons Learned:**

* A good upbringing did not save me from a life of addiction. It was something I was born with.
* Even though I had so much love in my life, I still grew up with immense insecurities, and they came along with me into adulthood.
* I didn't have to try so hard to fit in, I just had to learn how to be myself.

**Final Thoughts:**

Have you ever tried to be someone you're not, instead of accepting who you really are? Do you struggle to love yourself and still tell yourself the same stories from when you were a child?

Want to talk about it? info@theroadtohealth.me

**Suggested Solution:**

When I feel out of sorts or when I start to tell myself stories, I take 5 - 10 minutes and do a quick meditation or some reading. This practice helps to ground me.

* Meditation Practice
* Recommended Reading: The Gifts Of Imperfection - Brene Brown
* See Tips & Resources

## LIQUID GOLD

I grew up in an environment where alcohol wasn't a terrible thing. Some of my friends, on the other hand, did not have the same experience at home, which I thought was strange. To each their own I guess; we couldn't all have cool parents, right!? One evening I remember going to pick up a friend of mine well after her parents had fallen asleep. She was not allowed to go out late at night, and especially if that meant being around people who were drinking. After her parents had fallen asleep, she would try to sneak out. I watched from the car as she slipped out the front living room window. She was almost free when suddenly she was pulled back inside by her mother. I'm glad I could be honest and tell my parents where I went during my teenage years. Of course, I didn't always admit to what I was doing or that I was drinking, but my parents didn't have a problem with me going out for the night, which meant I did not have to sneak around.

The first time I got drunk, my friends and I ended up getting some beer and wine coolers. I had chosen wine coolers for my selection of beverages that evening because the alcohol content was 7%, as opposed to the lower percentage beer provided. It felt like a no brainer because you got more buzz for your buck. I poured myself a glass from the two-liter bottle, and off I went. I remember the feeling as though it was yesterday. That first drink gave me this sense of comfort like no other, and suddenly I felt more relaxed. Everything seemed brighter, and I felt like my world went from black and white to color. The shy, intimidated girl that I had become vanished. I was always so nervous about standing up for myself in fear of being judged. That all changed as I made my way through that two-liter bottle of liquid gold. Everything seemed right in the world. Ok, as a side note, let me say that even though I fell in love with alcohol that night only a few short months later, I would feel nauseated by certain flavors of wine coolers because of the quantity I had consumed. To this day, I still cannot drink peach flavored beverages just to give you an idea. I was ready to live life and stop feeling like the insecure girl that I had become, and alcohol gave me the confidence that I had been looking for. I had arrived!

The first time I remember blacking out was when I went camping with a friend and his family. We had started the trip just outside a small town about four hours away from where I lived. Basically, it was in the middle of nowhere, and to call it a town was an overstatement. It had one store and a handful of homes nearby. The store was a liquor store and a grocery store combined, which was the perfect combo if you ask me. Even though I couldn't buy booze myself because I was only 15, I was lucky that my friend's parents were relaxed and allowed us to get some beer and coolers. We started drinking in the afternoon, so by the time early evening rolled around, we were out of beverages, and no one would drive us back into town to grab more.

My friend decided that we would hang out with some of his older friends that evening. They were camping with the rest of the group but had their own area on the property. They were all in their late teens and early twenties, so my friend figured they would have some extra booze to share with us since we were all out. As we walked down to the fire, I heard music blasting, and it was Pearl Jam's album 10, which would become my favorite drinking album of all time. We listened to that CD on repeat over and over that night, and in all honesty, still to this day, when I hear a Pearl Jam song, it reminds me of that weekend. Sometime around midnight, I stood up and realized just how drunk I was. I had consumed a lot of alcohol before but hadn't blacked out yet at this point. One of the guys from the group we were hanging out with, who was clearly older than I was, started flirting a little. I loved the attention because he was cute, so I played it off like I was older than I really was. I don't think either of us disclosed our age that night, to be honest.

After more than a few drinks, we went up to my tent to be alone. As we made out, the world started to spin. I no longer felt as though I was on solid ground and needed to get outside quickly. Looking back, this would be the one, and only time I would be grateful that alcohol stopped me from making a terrible mistake. Not only was this guy 20 years old, and I was a minor, but I was also still a virgin and didn't want to lose my virginity being as wasted as I was. I got sick a few times, but I think he was just as drunk as I was, so he was kind enough to stick it out with me and hold my hair back. I remember going back to the fire and having a few more drinks, but everything else after that was a blur. The next thing I remember was that I woke up in between where the fire was located, and my tent, and I was looking up at the morning sky. As I slowly opened my eyes, the light made my head start to pound. I sat up and looked around to see where I was; I noticed some guys passed out around the fire behind me and my tent straight ahead, exactly how I had left it the night before. Apparently, I had attempted to get to my tent that night but never made it. From what I heard, I was a good time and really came out of my shell. This was just a preview as to how many of my evenings would end in the future. It was a weekend I would remember for a long time, and even though I got super sick and blacked out, I still enjoyed the feeling that alcohol gave me. A few months later, I ended up running into the guy I had messed around with when I was at the mall with a friend. When he noticed me, he looked over and said a quick hello as he walked by. Obviously, he realized how old I was after the fact and the mistake he almost made because he looked very uncomfortable running into me. The power of alcohol is a scary thing sometimes. Not that it should serve as an excuse, but I can give you plenty of stories where had I been in the same situation but sober, there is no way my actions would have carried out.

Until I started drinking and using drugs, my early teens had not been super eventful. I was a decent student, didn't skip class, and did my homework. Well, that all changed after I started drinking. I skipped class regularly, stole jewelry whenever I was at the mall, went home during the day when my parents weren't around to have a few drinks. I would even take lawn ornaments from homes around the neighborhood because I thought it was funny. When I needed money for booze, and I didn't have anything to sell, I took it from my mother's purse. I would just wait until I knew my Dad had given her some more cash and slide out a twenty occasionally, hoping she wouldn't notice. I would also go out with friends and break into cars, grab anything loose so we could sell it for cash. This behavior funded my drinking and drug use back then before I started working. I'm glad those days were short-lived, and I would soon get a job to support my habits.

The day I turned sixteen, I decided it was time to get my learner's license. Getting from one party to another party became hard because everyone lived so far apart, and the best house parties happened out in the middle of nowhere. My Dad would take me out driving a lot, and I made it through my thirty days before I went back down to the motor vehicle branch and took the driver's exam. To my amazement, I passed the first time around and was super excited to be handed my official driver's license. I was so proud, and I couldn't wait to get home and call my friends. That Saturday, I asked my mom if I could borrow her car to go visit a friend for the evening, and she agreed but told me to not be too late. I had the advantage of my parents going to sleep early, so they never greeted me at the door when I came home. That night I went over to my friend's place, and we had a couple of drinks before heading out. Back then, you always wanted to make sure you had a few drinks in you, so when you showed up at the party, you were already primed. We walked inside, and the party was already in full swing. People were dancing and having fun. Occasionally we would head outside to my mom's car and pile in together to smoke a few joints. Hot boxing made the experience that much more enjoyable, and I always came prepared with some air fresheners, so my mom would never know. We went back inside to join the party, and I went looking for a friend. When I walked into the basement, I thought maybe I was just super high and not seeing this right, but there she was with a brown paper bag to her mouth, inhaling whatever was inside the bag. Little did I know that there were actually more ways to get stoned than just your traditional methods. People would spray the contents of the aerosol can into a brown paper bag and then inhale to ingest whatever it was they sprayed into it. It didn't make much sense to me, and I was a little too wasted to partake in this adventure, so I went back upstairs. By this point, we were all pretty drunk, so a friend offered me something that might help straighten us out a little for the ride home later. It usually never took much convincing for me to try anything, so I took the pills. I swallowed them down, and I asked, "So what are these?" and to that, I was told, "Speed, it will help you with the effects of the alcohol." In hindsight, I probably should have asked what the pills were before taking them, but anytime I was super drunk, my decision-making skills lacked. The party continued, and I noticed I had a lot more energy than I did before, I felt great! One of my friends came over to me and started talking nonstop; at least it felt like that. I must have looked like a deer caught in the headlights because she paused, and we both broke out in laughter. My senses were heightened, and I didn't really notice that I was drunk anymore, so of course, I kept on drinking. I felt like I could go out and run a marathon, but yet all I could do is stand there and take it all in. A friend of mine decided she wanted to dance and got some people rounded up to join her. She was having the greatest time, even if it was by herself, and all I could do was sit and laugh. I was on the couch listening to music and hanging out, just taking it all in one minute, and suddenly the next thing I knew, I was sitting in the same room with the music turned off, and my friend was calling over for a sandwich in the kitchen. I felt so strange because one minute I was laughing at her dancing to loud music and the next I was sitting in a quiet room not sure what happened in between those two moments in time. What in the hell happened? I thought to myself. I figured now was a good time to head home, so I rounded up a few of my friends and told them I was heading out. I shouldn't have gotten in the car in the state I was in, but this shit was really freaking me out, and I wanted to make sure I got home ok. My mom had a Nissan Micra, which had about enough room to fit five people. Somehow, we got ten people in that car because a few people were left stranded at the party with no ride home. I drove back into town slowly; after all, I was only sixteen years old and had just received my license. The last thing I wanted was to get caught with ten people in the car or being drunk and high. As I drove slowly with my hands at the ten and two positions on the steering wheel with white knuckles, I made my way down the back roads. People were hanging all over each other in the car, so it was hard not to be distracted, but I tried to maintain what I thought was laser focus and amazing driving. One of my friends leaned in from the back through the middle of the console and kept me calm by repeating how great I was doing. It was pitch black, and the road felt narrow. As we drove down the road, a raccoon ran out in front of us suddenly, but it was too late for me to stop in time. My friend leaning through the front screamed, "Raccoon!!!!!" and suddenly the screams from the rest of the car were deafening. I slammed on the breaks to avoid the animal, but it was too late. There was a loud thud, and the screams in the car continued, as we came to a screeching halt. Thank god everyone was packed in so tightly that no one moved or got hurt. Of course, no one wanted to get out of the car to confirm the status of the raccoon. After some debate and me deciding that I didn't want to get caught in this situation, we drove off. I dropped everyone off and headed over to my friend's place for a couple of hours before heading home. As long as I was home before my parents woke up, I knew I would be in the clear, I just needed the effects of the speed and alcohol to wear off a little by smoking a couple of joints to calm down. We walked around to the front of the car to make sure there was no visible damage. The car itself was ok, but there was a little blood on the front bumper. We took a hose to make sure the evidence was washed away and left it at that. Unfortunately, I'm sure that the raccoon suffered a terrible fate that night and trust me when I say I thought about that night for a very long time afterward.

On Monday morning, I headed off to go to school. I met up with a friend in the hallway after the first period, and we hung out in our usual spot with a group of friends to discuss the events of the weekend. I told them that my mom was super pissed with me for putting the air-fresheners in her car after I had gotten home to disguise the smell of the weed. We traded stories back and forth when suddenly in mid-conversation; I experienced another blackout like I had the night of the party. One minute I was listening to friends chat about their evening, and the next, I was watching them walk away. One of my friends said, "Tamar! Wake up, are you coming?" I jumped off the bench and grabbed my stuff. You would assume occasions like these would smarten me up a little, but they did not. Imagine just sitting around having a conversation with friends, and for a short time, you remember nothing. The strange part is that for a full year after, any time I smoked pot, I would experience these short blackouts.

Until about 9th grade, I had done relatively well academically. This all changed when I started to drink, of course. My grades dropped, and I failed my math class, which my parents weren't super impressed by. I got put into a particular type of class for people who struggled in math. I have to be honest, I really enjoyed this class because it didn't take as much work to do well and the teacher gave us good grades no matter how we were doing. I realize now that this was the time in my life that I started to look at myself as someone who wasn't as smart as everyone else. This just added to the voices in my head that told me I wasn't good enough or smart enough. It gave me a perfect excuse to not try as hard, but in all reality, I didn't care anymore. I enjoyed the reputation I was starting to develop. Getting kicked out of class and being the class clown brought along with it some popularity and attention, so why on earth would I focus on getting my grades up? I signed up for a computer class, and the best part was that I didn't have to try all that hard to do well. I was already reasonably good on a computer, and so I would spend most of my time playing solitaire and asking random questions during class to give our teacher the impression that I was listening. As she would spend the time to answer my question, I would carry on playing my game. This also made a lot of my classmates laugh because I sat in the middle of the room, so everyone behind me could see what I was doing. I also met my friend Bev during this class. I now realize that people come into our lives for a reason, and Bev was one of those people. She would help to change my path several times over the next twenty years, although I didn't know it back then.

I had seen Bev in school before, but we had never become friends because we ran in different circles. I had always thought she might be a snob because she hung out with people whom I perceived were the cool kids, but once I got to know her, I realized that my opinion had been so far from the truth. Bev was one of the kindest people I got to know in high school. We ended up having our first couple of classes together that year, so we got to know each other well. After a brief time, we became close friends and were inseparable. This was a very positive thing for me because it drew me away from the crowd I was hanging out with that got me into so much trouble. It was only a matter of time before things would have gotten completely out of hand, so this new friendship was a blessing for me. Although I didn't stop drinking and many nights, Bev would be the person who was looking out for me when I was too drunk to drive and go home, it was still better than where I was heading before that. I really enjoyed that last year of school, and I would say it was probably my most memorable. I knew things were about to change, as we had to think about our future and decide what we wanted to do after graduation. There were decisions to make, and I had no idea what those were. All I knew was I didn't want the fun to end.

Graduation came fast, and I was asked to prom by a friend of mine, which was nice because there would be no pressure, and I knew it would be a good time. On the evening of our graduation ceremony, my Dad took me to the bank machine and gave me some money for the weekend festivities. As we walked in, he looked at me and told me he was proud of me and all I had accomplished. I gave him a big hug and thanked him for his support because it seemed like the right thing to say. I could tell though that something was wrong. He didn't look like himself, and there appeared to be a little more emotion in his eyes than usual. My Dad had always taught me to be strong, and so I never really showed my feelings. The funny thing is my Dad and I are very much alike and both emotional people. We are also both really passionate, which I wouldn't come to realize for some time yet. I didn't know it at that moment, but the reason my Dad was emotional that day was that he and my mom weren't doing so well, and I believe he had plans to leave after I graduated. I could see the strain in their relationship for a while now. I felt terrible for my mom because she did her best to be there for my brother and me and to make sure we were always happy. I loved both of my parents very much, although I'm sure I didn't always show it. I was more concerned about my social life as a teenager, so worrying about my parents was not high on my list. Regardless, I went out and enjoyed my graduation weekend and tried not to let anything else bother me.

My mom took my brother and I out to Edmonton, Alberta, right after grad for a couple of weeks to visit some old family friends. I always enjoyed going, but this time it was different because I felt as though there were a lot of things going on with my parent's marriage, and I didn't understand why my Dad wasn't coming along for our trip. Right before we returned home, I remember my Dad calling my mom and letting her know that he had been in a car accident. He wasn't seriously hurt, but my mom's car was totaled. We drove home shortly after that call, and when we got there and walked in the front door, I saw some of my Dad's stuff packed up and lying on the basement floor. I walked upstairs to unpack and didn't really understand what was going on. My mom came into my room with tears in her eyes. She sat down and told me that my Dad had left. I was devastated, although I had an idea that this might be happening a few weeks earlier. I had a great relationship with my Dad because of our years in soccer together, but I had a feeling that this would change. My mother was a stay at home mom for the most part unless she was working for my Dad. After my Dad left, I started to defend my mom because I saw how much this hurt her. Even though I loved my Dad dearly, it was my mother who I would stand by for the next few years.

Up until that time, I had played soccer and done really well at it. Now without my Dad around, things were changing. I was hanging out at home one evening with a friend having a few drinks when the phone rang. When I answered it, it was the coach from the BC Woman Soccer team. He asked me if I would be interested in trying out as their starting goaltender because he had been scouting at one of our last games and liked what he saw. He said he was impressed with my skills and would love it if I came to try out for the team. Under normal sober circumstances, this would seem like an opportunity of a lifetime that no one in their right mind would pass up, but I had a nice little buzz going, so even though I said yes, it was just another good intention on my part. I told them I'd be there and wrote the address down on a piece of paper. After I hung up the phone, I looked over at my friend and said, "Let's celebrate!" We had a few more drinks and headed out to a friend's place. Needless to say, I never made it to the tryouts because it fell on a Sunday, and of course, I would be hungover as usual. Playing soccer as an adult was one of my dreams growing up because my Dad had groomed me to become an excellent player. The power addiction had over me was usually more potent than the power to make a smart choice for my future. It was easy to make good choices when I was sober, but as soon as I had that first drink, I didn't follow up with the correct action.

Many people I knew ended up going to college after school. My Dad pushed me to go to a local college, but in all honesty, I had no idea what I wanted to do, nor did I really want to go. After all, my Dad wasn't really in the picture anymore. We would go visit occasionally, but things weren't the same. My Dad offered to pay for half of my education, and as I felt I didn't have much choice, I signed up for criminology to get him off my back. I took a couple of courses that year to appease my Dad and worked the rest of the time because now my mom was telling me I needed to pay rent as well. The first time I went to class, it felt so strange. I didn't know anyone, and it was people of all ages attending. A friend of mine had a class that overlapped mine. During my break, we would meet up and head over to the pub across the street for some drinks. This became a regular habit, so I usually ended up missing the last half of my class. After all, once I had a few beers, my plans always changed. When the first semester was over, I got my grades back and, to no surprise, had failed one of my two classes. I got a letter in the mail shortly after this, which said I was on academic probation, and if I didn't re-take my course and get a passing grade, they would not allow me back in. I decided this was a sign that I didn't belong in college, so it was time to move on. I felt as though I was chasing something that wasn't there. I had no desire to learn and had no idea what I wanted to do with my life, so the logical solution was to quit and solidify the belief I wasn't smart enough once again.

I had been in several relationships throughout high school, but I had a rule that they could only last for four months. This also included the guy I lost my virginity to, although he was great, and we had a lot of fun together. I figured that the best part of a relationship was the first few months. After that, you were at risk of things becoming boring or either of you getting too clingy. This strategy worked out fantastic for me because I didn't get attached to anyone, and they weren't too heartbroken when I broke up with them. I even did this with the guy I lost my virginity to! Typically, I would date people at least 19 years of age so they could buy me booze because even though I was 18 now, I still looked like I was about 12 years old. I had a fake ID once, and the first time I tried to use it, the bouncer looked at me and laughed. So needless to say, I had to be creative on how I got my booze and dating guys who were older than I was worked well for me. I had one relationship that lasted a full year, and I was proud of that, but again it got boring, so I knew it had to end. I was reasonably happy living my life this way. It always kept things exciting and fed my need for attention. Most times, right before I left a guy, I already had someone else in sight. It was almost like a game I played. I tried to stay single for a little just before I would turn 19, but that was short-lived.

One summer, after being newly single again, I met Tyler. A

friend of mine had met this guy, and she needed a wing woman for the evening. I wasn't about to say no to a good party, so I was happy to join her. I stood there having some drinks in the kitchen and talking to some new friends I met that night when Tyler walked right up to me and said, "Hello, nice to meet you! I'd like to get to know you more, but I have to run right now!" Just as quickly as he entered the room, he left, and my friend and I laughed at each other. Well, it turns out that I would meet Tyler again because one of his friends got in touch with me the following week to set up a date. That summer became one of the endless parties and a lot of enjoyable times. Tyler drank almost as much as I did, so that worked out nicely, and frequently he would just show up at my work and take me off for a weekend of fun with him and his friends. I remember one afternoon as I was working and just about to leave for the day one of my coworkers told me there was a motorhome full of people yelling my name out in the parking lot. Tyler then came into the restaurant and told me he had stopped by my house to grab some clothes and that we were heading out camping for the weekend. I got into the motorhome and was excited for what was about to take place. The party was in full swing, and my friend was also invited along, which made it even better. This was fairly common with Tyler's friends, and I didn't mind at all because I fit right in. Tyler and I became very close that summer, and our relationship started to get more serious, so we talked about possibly moving in together. He was finishing up a couple of years at a community college, so after that, he could head off to university for a few more years and finish up his bachelor's degree in engineering. I felt fortunate to land a guy that not only partied like I did but also had a future ahead of him. Unfortunately, both of us started to develop control issues, and those issues would begin to affect our relationship.

There were small signs I would often ignore. Even though we partied together a lot, I think it wore on Tyler quickly. He had a lot of insecurities, and frankly, I didn't care at the time. I felt that this was his problem to deal with but also didn't realize how this behavior would trigger my own insecurities. I had never been the jealous type, but when he started to display these signs, I came right back with my own. He tried to control when I went out and who I went out with, and I can't say I blamed him because it was easy for me to get in trouble. He didn't trust a lot of my friends, and to be honest, I did not trust any of his. I recall one evening I was planning to go out with some friends for dinner and drinks. I had planned on having a night out for my birthday, but Tyler called me and warned me against drinking too much because he had a special weekend away planned, and he didn't want me to ruin it by being super hungover. I was angry that he was trying to tell me what to do, but I kept things low key that night. Tyler also had plans to go to a gig where one of his friends was playing downtown that same evening. Apparently, he offered to be the designated driver for the night. The thing was that Tyler and his friends never took it easy, and so I had a gut feeling his promise wasn't going to be kept.

The following day I called Tyler at lunch to find out what time he wanted me to come over so we could head out for our weekend away. When his mom answered the phone, she told me Tyler was still sleeping. I was livid, so I left work early and headed over to his place to find out what had happened. Sure enough, he had gone out and apparently gotten so drunk he didn't even remember getting home. The sad part was he wasn't even sure if he had driven or not. His truck was a mess, and this was the way we started off my birthday weekend. This kind of behavior became pretty standard in our relationship. Each of us was trying to control the other and doing more damage than good. I became vindictive and would do things to purposely hurt Tyler because there was no way I would let someone else control me. You would think at this point one of us would end things for each other's sanity, but that's not what you do when you're both codependents of one another. Instead, I decided I would follow him as he went off to university, and we would see if living together would fix all our problems. This is when things really took a turn for the worst.

**Lessons Learned:**

* Before you put anything in your body, make sure you know what it is first!
* Driving around with ten people in a small car is not safe.
* Music has always stirred up memories or emotions for me. Today when I struggle with feelings, I turn on a good song.
* Even though it took time, I had to learn how to eliminate the emotions of jealousy and envy from my life and replaced them with trust and gratitude.
* Numbing out my feelings never made them go away. Instead, they got worse until I learned to feel them.

**Final Thoughts:**

Have you ever found yourself engaging in addictive behavior to numb your feelings and just forget? Maybe it's been with drugs or alcohol, or perhaps it's even been with food? You are not alone, and if you want to share that experience with someone who understands, let me know.

You can email me at info@theroadtohealth.me

**Suggested Solution:**

Find help through the many programs that are available for people who suffer from addiction.

## WHAT MORALS?

When Tyler and I decided to move in together, we assumed this would fix all the things that were terribly broken with our relationship. Boy was I ever wrong, but we'll get into that shortly. Tyler was heading over to the island to go to university, so I figured it would be a great time to move out of my mom's place and go live on my own. I had a friend that lived on the island, so I knew I would have someone to hang out with other than just Tyler. The first month of our time on the island was a little rocky. Tyler and I were used to partying together, but a lot of things changed when he decided to grow up and go to university. It was time for him to get serious, but that was of no interest to me. So while he spent his time getting educated, I got a job and made some new friends. Most of my weekends were spent at the bar having fun, which Tyler didn't like all that much. I didn't understand why he would get so bent out of shape when I went out with friends; after all, he was the one going to school, not me. I guess there comes a time with most people that do not suffer from addiction that they decide to grow up and make something of themselves. I had already tried going to college, and it didn't work out, so I was determined to enjoy life. I also didn't care that my behavior was starting to affect our relationship in such a negative way. I remember coming home from the bar one night, and when I went to open the door, Tyler had put the chain on so I wasn't able to get in. He left me out in the hallway of our apartment for what felt like an hour. I felt as though Tyler was becoming a little too controlling over how I spent my time, and that didn't really fly with me.

Things went on like this for the next few months. I spent most weekends at the bar with friends enjoying myself while he studied at home. I would do the complete opposite of what he asked of me, and this just pissed him off even more. Even though I had made some fantastic friends on the island, I started to go back home every couple of weekends because I was getting homesick as well as tired of fighting all the time. After a couple months of traveling back and forth, I finally told Tyler I was moving back to the mainland. I didn't want to fight anymore, and I thought it would be best for him to finish his university degree without me there as a distraction. I also never felt truly at home living together, so I figured it was the best thing for both of us.

I ended up calling my friend Liz whom I used to work with, and we decided to get a place together because she was looking to get out of her parent's house. I would still talk to Tyler occasionally but was having a lot more fun hanging out with friends in the evening than worrying about my relationship. I think I was just afraid to end up alone and single, so I kept Tyler around for the comfort of having someone to fall back on, although now I realize what a terrible mistake that was. Plus, to be fair, he was a great guy. I just didn't appreciate it at the time, and I think we both needed to spend some time being single to figure out who we were. Regardless, when I moved back, I needed a night out, so I called up some old friends. We ended up at a restaurant that was relatively new and popular in town. One of my friends had just started dating a car salesman at the time, and this guy was super generous with his money, which was good because I didn't have any. He paid for dinner, drinks, and of course, drove us around in his brand new work vehicle. I was impressed, but then again, I was impressed by anyone willing to supply me with my beverages for the evening. After we finished up dinner, I decided it was a good idea to kick it up a notch, so I ordered some shots. My idea of kicking it up a notch also involved table dancing and flashing the entire restaurant, which some of the guests didn't appreciate too much apparently. The owners, although entertained, told us we had to wrap things up before others decided to partake in the nudity. I was pretty close to blackout at this point but knew our evening had only begun. I went out to the parking lot and made myself get sick. I figured that if I could get rid of some of the alcohol in my system, I could last a little longer. We headed on over to a new night club that had just opened and continued our evening there. I loved to get out and dance when I had the chance, and because our whole evening was being paid for, I enjoyed it even more. A couple hours later, however, I was having some trouble getting around, according to my friends. One of the guys called a cab for me because clearly, I wasn't going to last much longer. I got in the taxi and vaguely remembered the driver asking me where I lived. This is where my memory of that evening ends. I woke up the next morning in bed with a bucket on the floor beside me. As I tried to sit up, there was a knock on my door. Liz walked in and asked, "How was your evening?" I had no idea how I ended up home because the last thing I remember was getting into the cab. Liz told me that at a certain point, the cab driver had gotten so fed up with my inability to tell him where I lived that I called her and passed over the phone so she could explain. This would be the start of many evenings like this.

I was having the time of my life, and with Tyler out of sight, I felt like there was no pressure to behave myself. One evening I went out to a pub with a few friends and ran into a guy I went to elementary school with. Nick and I had spoken a few times through a mutual friend over the years, but it was a long time since I'd seen him. We had a few drinks together, and by the end of the evening, I was feeling pretty good. We went back to our friend's place to have a nightcap, and as neither of us was in any shape to drive, we ended up crashing on the floor in the living room together. We talked for a while and then ended up hooking up. When Nick felt he was ok to drive, he offered me a ride home as we lived right down the street from each other coincidentally. As he dropped me off, he said, "We should do this again sometime." I agreed, got out of the car, and said goodbye. As I laid in bed that night, the memories of the evening put a smile on my face. I felt like a giddy schoolgirl just having her first kiss again, but there was only one problem, I was still in a relationship with Tyler.

Tyler came over the following weekend to visit, and it was nice to see him, although my mind was on Nick. I had seen Nick a couple more times since our first night together, so it was hard to get him off my mind. He was such a great guy and so much fun to hang out with. I did the best I could to give Tyler my full attention when he came to visit, but it wasn't easy. I also started to feel a little guilty about what I was doing. Tyler would often call when I was out, and because I was at the bar a lot with friends, he started to get angry when he could never get a hold of me. I'm not sure why I hadn't ended my relationship with Tyler yet because it really wasn't fair. I think it was just more comfortable for me to avoid.

Tyler was in town one weekend and asked if we could

hang out. I told him I was busy, but that maybe we could connect the following day. I had plans with Nick that night, so I figured I could see both of them that weekend. I didn't spend the night at Nick's place but left around 4am to go home so I could get some sleep. A few hours later, I was met with a knock at the door and an angry boyfriend. He burst into the house and started asking me who Nick was. I was still half asleep and told him I had no idea what he was talking about. Apparently, Tyler had figured out the code to my voicemail and checked my messages. A friend of mine had left me a voicemail that night asking me if I was with Nick. She then proceeded to tell me to make sure I called her the following day with all the details. Now would have been an excellent time to come clean and finally start being honest with Tyler because that was what he deserved. Instead, I was furious that he had hacked my phone, so of course, instead of telling him the truth, I lied and told him it was a joke and then stated that our relationship was over. We had been growing apart now for several months, but it still didn't excuse my behavior. Tyler was a great guy and was really determined to make something of himself, I was just not in a place to be with someone like that back then. I would later discover that one of my biggest fears was the fear of abandonment. I didn't like to be alone with myself, and it was something that made me very uncomfortable, so I would hold onto relationships much longer than I should have.

After Tyler and I officially broke up, Nick and I realized we didn't want to jeopardize our friendship by getting into a serious relationship, so we remained friends. I also thought it might be a good idea for me to stay single for a while as I really hadn't spent much time doing so. I would spend time hanging out with my roommate and other friends. One afternoon I decided to go visit Liz and grab some lunch where she worked. One of the delivery drivers stopped in, and because I had worked there years prior, I was familiar with him. He was about 10 years older than I was and had this charming personality that just drew me to him. It had been years since we'd seen each other, so that afternoon, he walked up to me and called me by the nickname he had come up with 3 years earlier. "Hey, Peppermint Patty! How the hell are you??" He came over and gave me a big hug which of course I enjoyed because not only was he super funny but he was very handsome. And yes, if you're wondering where the nickname came from, just look up my picture, then go check out the Charlie Brown characters, and you'll see why. Pep is still one of the nicknames people call me today. We stood at the back of the restaurant with Liz chatting it up for about 30 minutes before he let us know he had to head out for his next delivery. I was disappointed, and I could tell my roommate was as well because talking to Adam was always a pleasure. As he hopped into his truck, he looked over and said, "Hey, Pep, find me on messenger and let's chat one night." Off he went and all I could think of the rest of the afternoon was getting home so we could chat a little more. Of course, it wasn't the same at seeing him in person, but I felt as though we had a connection, and I was super excited about it.

That evening I went out with some friends as I usually did, but I was more excited to get home so I could hop online and get to know Adam a little better. After all, I could always have some drinks, head home early, and avoid waking up somewhere, not entirely sure of how I got there in the first place. This was a common occurrence because most of the evenings that I went out to the bar, I ended up in a blackout. I grabbed a beer and a piece of leftover pizza and sat down to turn on the computer. I signed into messenger and waited for Adam to join. Not long after, I got a message, and all of a sudden, I got butterflies in my stomach. We chatted for what felt like hours that evening. In the beginning, it was an innocent conversation, but towards the end, I felt as though there was a little flirting going on, and I really liked it.

A few days later, Adam and I decided to meet up for a drink. He was incredibly flirty and kept reaching under the table and putting his hand on my leg as we chatted. I enjoyed some beers and started to get a bit of a buzz going on. I was having a hard time focusing on our conversation because I couldn't help but wonder what it would be like to hook up with him. Adam asked if I wanted to go somewhere where we could be alone, and of course, I agreed right away, so we decided to head on over to his place. He told me he had the house to himself for a few hours, so we were all good. Now, this is the point where I should have walked away; after all, I knew he had been in a relationship when I first met him 3 years earlier but should have asked if he was still in that relationship today. I had the feeling that he was, but I was enjoying the attention, so I wasn't really thinking that someone else may get hurt as a result of my actions. Adam was such a flirt that you would have assumed he was single, and I would soon find out that, in fact, he was actually married and also had a child recently. For some reason, this still didn't seem to stop him from wanting to take this further. We arrived at his place, and he grabbed me a beer while he gave me a tour. When we hit the bedroom, he grabbed my beer and put it down. We started to make out, and before I knew it, we were doing everything except having sex. I didn't understand why at first, but then he told me there was a limit to what he would do because of his marriage. For some strange reason, I accepted that as an answer, and instead of calling things off as I should have, I decided to carry on this little affair. After all, I was having my needs met, it was nothing serious, and I was getting the attention

I craved. He would often show up at my work, and we would go park at the back of the parking lot so we could go make out in my car. Needless to say, I was enjoying all the attention I was getting from this man.

I was never very good with money, so there were times I had trouble paying bills and covering my extracurricular activities. I went to my mom's place to do my laundry because then I could also ask her for money so I could afford to buy booze. I had been navigating through life and using others to support my habits and needs. One of these occasions I had big plans to go out to the new club in town with some friends. I was hanging out at home and had a few beers but didn't have any money to spend that evening. I started to panic a little because the last thing I wanted was to cancel out; after all, I was the life of the party, and the party couldn't go on without me. Just then, Adam called. He had been out all day with his buddies and sounded a little drunk, which I thought was kind of funny because he was flirting even more than usual. After asking what I was doing, I told him what my potential plans were but that I was a little broke at the moment, so trying to figure out a solution. Adam said he may have a solution for me and told me he was coming over for a drink. When he arrived, he had a case of beer with him, which I was super grateful for because I was running out myself. After a few drinks, Liz decided to go to her room and give us some time alone. Adam looked over and said, "So you need some money, do you?" I nodded and gave him a smile because I honestly thought he would just give me some. He smiled back and said, "I know a way that would convince me to give you some if you're up to it?" This was the first time I started to feel a little uncomfortable around Adam. We had a lot of physical contact over the last few months, but the idea of giving sexual favors for the exchange of money wasn't something I had ever considered. I was desperate, though, and didn't see any other way, so I stuffed away what little morals I had left and obliged. He handed me forty bucks and thanked me for a beautiful evening, then kissed me goodbye. I felt dirty for what I had just done, so I needed to throw back a few more drinks to forget. I knew I had to end it because this wasn't a situation I wanted to put myself in again. After all, I had morals, right?

I decided that I was going to swear off any sort of relationship that summer, or so I thought. That promise to myself didn't last very long. After you've had a few drinks and someone happens to offer you some more, you don't say no; after all, that would just be rude, right? This started a summer of one night stands because if someone was going to spend their hard-earned money on showing me a good time, it was only fair that I could pay them back in a different way. Besides, I didn't want to get into anything serious because then it all became complicated, and that wasn't what I was looking for. Things went rather well for those first few months, but the mistake I soon made was taking advantage of guys I worked with, which made my work life a little awkward, to say the least. It wasn't always easy to face my victims the following day and have to explain that what happened the night before would never happen again. Of course, that was easy to say until we ended up together at an event with work friends, got drunk, and accidentally ended up hooking up for a second time. This was when I decided I had to make a few changes. I had moved twice during this period because apparently not paying your rent isn't something that most people appreciate. I found some new roommates where the rent would be cheaper and found a new job for the summer that would allow me to make a fresh start. I had to make some changes, but unfortunately, the ones I would soon make would lead me down an even darker path.

**Lessons Learned:**

* By holding onto my shame, I felt it only grew. I had to learn how to talk about it with someone I could trust to begin to let go.
* I thought that receiving a lot of attention from men meant that I was loveable. Instead, it made me feel used, so I had to learn to love myself.

* Moving in with someone when I wasn't ready just made things a whole lot worse.
* As a result of how dependant I was in most of my relationships, I would later learn how to become more independent and do things for myself. I set boundaries.

**Final Thoughts:**

Have you ever done anything that left you ashamed, and you haven't been able to talk about it? When we carry that burden on our own, it can get heavy. It's ok to set boundaries.

Share your story and begin to let go.
info@theroadtohealth.me

**Suggested Solution:**

When I find myself carrying around shame or guilt for something that I've done, I take one of two actions. For shame, I share this with someone I trust because it takes power away. When it comes to guilt, I determine if I owe an amends to someone and make it right away.

* Recommended Reading: The Gifts Of Imperfection - Brene Brown
* See Tips & Resources

## A LOWER LEVEL

In my early twenties, my party life was in full swing. I worked at a golf course for the summer, which worked out perfectly because they allowed me to drink during my shift. In fact, they encouraged it, which was a dream job for a person like me. A typical day at work meant arriving shortly before my shift started and doing a quick shot. I did a little cooking but mostly waitressing and handling the bar. After my shift ended, I would often hang out with the regulars and staff and play card games all evening long. After large tournaments, strippers were usually ordered, so that always made for an exciting evening. You could say there was never a lack of fun to be had.

One evening, my co-worker Lara and I left work and went to enjoy a few more drinks at my place. On the way, she asked me if we could make a quick stop to pick something up. I agreed and drove us out to a place out in the middle of nowhere. Lara asked me if I had ever done coke before, to which I responded, "No, but I've always wanted to try it. Is it like speed?" I asked. She said, "Sort of, but it's even better!" I was already somewhat drunk, so there wasn't much convincing me. I had seen cocaine before, but when we got back to my place, Lara pulled out a bag of what looked like little white rocks. She explained that it was coke but just cooked up into a form called crack, which made it easier to ingest because you could smoke it instead of snorting it. To be honest, I didn't really care what form it came in, as long as it made me feel good. My roommates were home at the time, and I had a feeling they wouldn't be super crazy about me smoking crack in the apartment or smoking it all, so we took it outside on the patio where we had a big comfy couch to hang out on.

Lara had made up a makeshift pipe from a pop can and explained how to smoke it. She put a small piece on the top of the pop can and passed it over. I was nervous but super excited at the same time. I had always wanted to try coke but didn't really know anyone who sold it.

I let out a deep breath to remove the air from my lungs and then put the can to my lips. I lit up the lighter and inhaled as deeply as I could, taking in all the smoke. Lara told me to hold my breath in for as long as I could before releasing, so that is what I did. I put my head back, and with a big slow breath out, I released. Instantly my body became lighter and my head clear. The feeling was one unlike I had ever felt before, my senses were at an all-time high. We spent the next hour chatting about our dreams and all the amazing things we would do with our lives while we continued to take hits off that pop can. I was feeling reasonably drunk before we started, and although I continued to drink while we smoked, I felt like I had control over the effects of the alcohol. I would typically hit a point in the evening where I blacked out, but not this time. Tonight there would be no consequences because of my drinking, or so I thought.

Cocaine had become my new drug of choice at that point. Lara and I smoked it many evenings in my room while my roommates were in the living room. We would play cards for hours on end until the sun came up, because let's be honest, even though I felt I had the energy to run a marathon in the middle of the night I sure as hell would not do so. The thing with crack is that once you take a hit, unlike doing a line of coke, it hits you instantly. There was no gradual high, it happened immediately. On the flip side, it also wore off a lot faster, so when you run out and start coming down again, it can feel like the worst experience in the world. There would be times we'd run out around midnight, which was way too early to stop, so we'd scrounge up any money we could and run out to our dealer who lived about thirty minutes out of town. Driving while high on crack was not fun. It is like having an experience where you just had the shit scared out of you, your heart is pounding, your eyes are wide open, and you're super aware of your surroundings but also paranoid. It was always like something out of a movie. We arrived at the dealer's place and went inside, but this time, unlike others we had picked up, several other people were hanging out getting high. I was so high myself, so I was in no position to judge anyone in the room, I just knew I needed to take a hit soon before the effects wore off any further, because the jaw-grinding was killing me. Although this memory is a blur, I remember seeing a woman sitting in the corner of the living room, and it looked as though she was pregnant. When you're high like this, it's hard to feel any emotion around seeing this sort of stuff. You only care about one thing, and nothing else seems to matter. This was not the first time I had witnessed this type of environment, nor would it be the last. We got our pipe ready quickly so we could get our fix and head back home.

As I share this story with you, it literally makes my gut hurt. I had such a great upbringing that it seemed very unlikely I would have to experience events like these in my adult life. After all, I should have gone to college, started a family, and bought a house, right? I'm here to tell you that when you react the way I do to drugs, alcohol, or any other substance at a certain point, you're not surprised by anything anymore. You lose all sense of control because, from the time you consume something, the only thing on your mind is how to get more. I mention this now because I think it's so important to be aware of if you don't understand. The cravings start after we take that first hit or drink, and from that point on, we lose complete control. Never in my life did I think I would be sitting in a crack house in the middle of the night using with other addicts because, in my mind, I was too good for this lifestyle. I'm certainly not proud of these times, but it has, however, helped to shape who I am today, and I'm stronger because of it.

Even though working at the golf course was super fun, it didn't exactly pay very well. Most of my paycheque went to paying off my bar tab, the balance went to my rent. I ate at the golf course most nights when I worked and then stocked up on Mr. Noodles and Kraft dinner for when I needed to eat at home. I got by, but with my newfound love for cocaine, I had to make more money. Sometimes to get by on the weekend, we would deposit one of my cheques into Lara's bank account. She would withdraw some cash, and then we would try to pay it back later, which rarely happened. This only lasted for so long before the bank decided I could no longer deposit cheques, so we had to find another way. I decided since it was the end of summer and the golf season was slowing down, I would go find an actual job. I reached out to a friend of mine I used to play soccer with, and she said there was an opening for an order picker at the place she worked. I sent in my resume, and she ended up giving me a great reference. This is something I would later regret because, as an addict, you seem to get very unreliable and tend to let people down. But needless to say, I got the job anyway, and I was super excited.

I woke up the first day of my new job filled with excitement, and I was eager to prove I could do the job well. I wasn't all that excited about the commute, but the money was good, and for the time being, it would support my lifestyle. I enjoyed the work for the most part and my hours were from 11 am to 7 pm, so it also allowed me to sleep in and avoid rush hour. The first month went reasonably well, and I kept myself out of trouble. I also met a guy that worked on the evening shift, and we flirted a bit here and there. Our schedules overlapped by a few hours, so I could always spend my last break with him. Sean and I started dating officially shortly after, and I have to say for the record that he was one of the kindest guys I'd ever been with, and I took full advantage of that. Unfortunately, during that time of my life, I was not in a headspace to treat him with respect like he deserved. I would stay over at his place most weekends that we had matching days off. Sean cooked for me and would lend me money when I didn't have enough to support my habit. The sad part is I would lie and tell him it was to pay my rent or bills. At the time, he filled the void of companionship in my life that I thought I was missing. Even though I wanted to be in a healthy relationship, I was more interested in getting drunk or high, so I used him much more than I am proud to say. He provided me what I needed, and I took advantage of that.

After a few months, I finally finished paying back the money I owed the bank for the bounced cheques. Lara and I decided this was cause to go out and celebrate. Even though I had to work the next day, we hit the bar that evening and brought some coke with us to add to the fun. By this time I wasn't picky with how I used, typically if we went to the bar or out with a group of friends, we would do lines because we thought it was the more classy way to consume coke, and when it was just the two of us hanging out and playing cards all night, we would fire up the pipe and smoke it. We had a blast that night; the drinks flowed, and the lines continued well into the morning. Somehow we ended up back at my place, and to be honest, I'm not all that sure how we got there, but I remember looking out the window and seeing the sun come up. Lara wasn't a big drinker, so she would usually end up driving us home if I was too wasted. I looked at my watch, and it was 6 am. "Shit, I really need to get some sleep so I can get up in a few hours and get to work!" I told Lara. We smoked a joint, hoping it could minimize some effects of my high so I could possibly fall asleep. A couple hours later, I realized I wasn't going to fall asleep anytime soon, so I reached for my phone and called in sick. This would be the first of many times over the next few weeks I called in.

My roommates were starting to wonder why I was missing work so much when it was clear I was out all night partying. I wanted to avoid any confrontation with them, so I decided I would be better off going to stay with Lara for the week. Her boyfriend was out-of-town, so we had the place all to ourselves. I had the following day off, so we decided we would grab more coke, food, and booze so we could have a card and movie night. I was super grateful I had the following day off because we never got to sleep until about 7 am the next morning. Unfortunately, my days off were spread out through the week. I had Tuesday and Saturday's off, so it made it harder for me to sustain my unhealthy lifestyle without effecting my employer due to my unreliability. The following evening we continued on with no worry about the fact that I had to work the next day. As usual, I called in sick, but this time, I used the excuse that someone in my family had passed. I had heard Lara use this excuse in the past and figured if it worked for her, it would work for me. I would never think about doing something like this today, but back then, it was easier to lie. I had been sick a few times in the weeks before, so I thought I was smart to come up with something new. Even though I felt guilty for this, I didn't want to show up at work and lift heavy objects with little to no sleep. This routine carried on for the next week straight. We had depleted all our money and had no idea what to do next. I decided it would be smart of me to go home that day and get some sleep as I felt like my body was about to shut down. I didn't have to work the following day, so I took the entire day to sleep before heading back after my week-long bender.

I woke up the next morning and looked in the mirror. My face was pale, and I looked like I was sick. Maybe this look would help convince my boss I had indeed been grieving the week I was away. When I arrived at work that morning, I said hello to everyone and started my shift. I was relieved there had seemed to be no consequences for my absence. As I moved around the warehouse picking up food and drink items to load on my pallet, I had an order that required five kegs of beer. Now usually, this wasn't an issue, but when you are fresh off a crack bender that lasted seven days, you're not exactly feeling strong. Instead of asking for help, which in hindsight I should have done, I tried to lift all five kegs on my own. As I hauled the last keg of beer up onto the pallet, I felt something in my back pull. It was a pain I've never experienced before, and it almost took my breath away. I made my way to the office and explained what happened. I could barely drive, so Sean took the afternoon off to take me to the doctor and allowed me to stay at his place. I woke up the next morning, barely able to get out of bed. After getting an x-ray and a check-up, I was told I had slipped a disk in my back and that I would need to rest for a few weeks. They also mentioned I would most likely be off work for the following few months and had to go to physiotherapy. They gave me pain meds and sent me on my way. I was told to file a claim so they would pay me while being off work, as this was a work-related injury. To my surprise, my pay would end up being more than it was when I was working. As you could probably imagine, this wasn't an ideal situation for an alcoholic like myself. I had three months off work, was getting paid more than my usual income without the worries of working for it. The bonus was that I had been given pain killers to help manage my pain! I really saw nothing wrong with this scenario, and now I had the time I needed to enjoy my life without the added responsibility of a job. Of course, the first couple of weeks sucked, but after I could get up and move around again, things were great!

The next three months were a blur. To be honest, all I remember was that I wanted to make the most of my time off. I was out with Lara and her boyfriend Kyle, making deliveries most nights. He sold weed at the time, so frequently Lara and I would tag along for the ride. He would supply us with enough beer for the entire evening, so we could drink on the way, and sometimes we would get out at his stops and mingle with the clients to socialize a little. We were usually drunk towards the end of his runs, so many times, we would grab some coke to straighten out a little, so he would be ok to drive. One of those evenings, we rented a motel room with an extra bedroom because we didn't feel like driving around anymore. Kyle had gotten us enough coke to last the whole evening. As we sat there in the room doing lines to our heart's content, Kyle took a quick shower. We played cards as usual and chatted away. For some strange reason, Kyle had decided to set up a tray to put all the coke on for safekeeping right outside the bathroom door. We failed to realize that as soon as Kyle opened that door, the steam from the shower would affect the nice powdery consistency of the coke. We heard Kyle shout, "For fucks sakes!!" He panicked and yelled at us to come and grab the tray. The beautiful powder had turned into a chunky mess. If you've ever tried cocaine before, you'd know that it's not exactly easy to just stop using if you have a bunch at your disposal, and if you're an addict like we were, quitting was not an option. We chopped it up as best as we could and just decided that the pain of snorting what felt like rocks up our noses would have to do. These types of evenings would become a common occurrence, and I hated hiding this from Sean. I often lied to him for obvious reasons where I was and what I was doing. I would disappear for a few days at a time and then come back when I was exhausted and needed a break.

After three months of being off work, I was told that I could go back. I wasn't all that excited about it, but I was also not in good shape at this point and incredibly worn out from the many nights of no sleep. I figured that going back to work was probably the best thing for me. Maybe I could straighten up a little and get back on track. Unfortunately, when I walked in that day after being off for three months, I found out I didn't have a job anymore. To be honest, I shouldn't have been surprised by this, but of course, I was and played the victim. I'm not sure if Sean and I broke up before this happened or after, and to be honest, I didn't even remember breaking up with him at all. He was an innocent victim during a not so glorious time in my life. That all being said, years later, I reached out to him to meet in person so I could make amends and own up to what I did. I paid him back the money I owed and apologized for treating him the way I did. I'm grateful that I have learned to take ownership of the things that I have done in the past. Although this didn't mend all the relationships I had harmed, it was a start.

Lara had become a big part of my life back then. We spent countless evenings getting high and drunk together, and looking back on this time, we did some pretty stupid shit. Just before she moved in with Kyle, she would stay at my place, and both my roommates loved her because she was a fantastic cook. I certainly don't regret everything we did because there were a lot of fun times that went along with the bad. The only problem was that both Lara and I suffered from addiction, so we only fueled each other's behavior. I hadn't even realized it at the time. But the first time we smoked crack together set Lara off on a path she had been down before. There were nights when Lara would disappear, and Kyle would call me to come help find her. You would think times like these would encourage me from using with her, but they didn't. I continued because I was only looking out for myself. Don't get me wrong, I cared about what was happening, but those feelings all went away after the first hit. When she told me she was ok, I would go along for the ride. No matter what happened, Kyle, Lara, and I always stuck together.

I remember one day Kyle had called me up and asked if I wanted to go help him look for a ring for Lara. I had nothing going on at the time because I wasn't working, so I agreed! Partway through our outing, his brother called and asked if we wanted to go out for lunch. We grabbed a case of beer on the way and decided to make a day of it. Kyle's brother brought a friend along with him, so all four of us agreed that it would be fun to head on over to one of our local strip joints. We had a blast hanging out, playing pool and drinking the afternoon away. The strippers were friendly, and as long as we made it back in time to pick Lara up from work, we were all good. Shot after shot came our way because Kyle was feeling generous that day as he had just picked up a ring for Lara a few hours prior, so it was time to celebrate. Unfortunately, our celebration would end up with us getting kicked out of the bar. I had just ordered another pitcher of beer when I heard the bouncer yell at us to leave. I wasn't going anywhere without that full pitcher of beer, so I did what any alcoholic would do and tucked the beer under my arm and ran like hell. There was no way I was wasting this liquid gold! I made it to the car just in time before the bouncer could catch up to me, and we drove away. We had to jump on a ferry to cross the river to get home, so we shared the rest of the beer. While sitting in the car, some young punks had made some comments at us. Kyle had a hard time keeping his mouth shut and tried to put them in their place by saying a few choice words. This banter went on for the next ten minutes, and we didn't think much of it. The ferry ride was brief, and after we were exiting the ferry and headed towards home, we didn't realize the police were waiting there for us. This might have worked out ok if it wasn't for the two pounds of weed in the trunk that Kyle failed to tell us about. None of us knew this, but when they got Kyle out of the car to give him a breathalyzer, they had opened the trunk and removed the two bags of weed from the back. Kyle's brother, his friend, and I were pulled out of the car, thrown on the ground and handcuffed. We heard Kyle's phone ringing nonstop, but because they cuffed us, no one could answer. I assumed it was Lara and that she wasn't all that impressed we hadn't shown up yet. We were supposed to pick her up from work that afternoon, but instead, Kyle was being hauled off to jail. It's not all that fun having to explain to your best friend why you didn't show to pick her up and how her boyfriend landed in jail. After she had finished yelling at us, we headed over to the police station, where they released Kyle on bail. Lara was so angry she started yelling at both of us, and I can't say I blamed her. Kyle turned around and threw the ring he had bought her at her feet from what I can remember. Needless to say, it was a quiet ride home.

I didn't realize it back then, but for things to change when it comes to addiction, you had to actually accept that you have a problem in the first place. I had been fired from two different jobs because of my behavior, and I still never recognized that anything was wrong. I didn't always like the situations I got myself into, but this became my new norm.

**Lessons Learned:**

* Addiction can come in many forms. Some people lean towards one, but I learned that for me to use one often means using more.
* Once I take that first drink, the power of choice goes away, and I don’t take the possible consequences into

consideration.
* I had to learn to confront the guilt that troubled me for the things I had done. Then I had to make amends to all of those I effected to move forward. The guilt did not go away until I faced it.

**Final Thoughts:**

* Have you ever reached a point where you felt so out of control that you had no idea how to stop? There is a way out.

Email if you can relate: info@theroadtohealth.me

**Suggested Solution:**

Addiction is a serious problem. Find help through the many available programs. Do not wait until it's too late!

* Meditation & Prayer

## HOW DID I GET HERE?

I had been single for some time now, so I figured I needed to get back into the market. That following year is when I met Tim. I was over at a friend's place doing some day drinking, and he was doing some yard work for them. He kept glancing over at us but didn't say much, only smiled once in a while. After he was done, he came over to join us for a drink. He seemed very shy, so I asked my friend Amber what his deal was. She told me he had struggled with addiction and was finally getting his life together, so they got him to do certain things around the house for some extra money. After Amber mentioned this, I couldn't help but wonder what the hell he was doing over here because most evenings spent with Amber and her husband ended up with us doing coke.

To give you an idea of how bad it was, we often went to the bar but spent a lot of time in the bathroom stall doing line after line. Many evenings we would continue on long after the bar closed. One of those evenings, we went over to a friend's place to keep the party going. I'm not sure why but because we were all super high, we decide to go have a naked hot tub together. Although that night was a bit of a blur, I remember very clearly that Amber's husband was having sex with another woman right in front of us all.

Amber had gone back inside to do another line, so she had no idea what was going on. I decided it was time to get out to give them some privacy. As I tried to escape the hot tub, I slipped and ended up doing a face plant on the wooden deck below. I wasn't wearing any clothes, so it wasn't my proudest moment, but I believe I left with only some bruises and a sore ego. These types of evenings weren't all that uncommon with Amber and her husband. I remember another one of these evenings we ended up at an after-hours hells angels bar where I mingled with the local bikers for a few hours. I also remember Amber wanting to leave, so I decided I was just going to get a ride home, not all that smart, but then again, I didn't often make the right decisions while I was drunk and high. So, as you can see, I didn't understand what Tim was doing hanging out with two people that did what he was trying to recover from.

The afternoon Tim and I met, we got to know each other a little. He told me a little about his history and that he had been clean for a few months now. I congratulated him and wished I could have said the same, but instead, I told him that I was a casual user, and it's never been a big deal for me. Oh, the lying was starting already, and we had only known each other for a few hours. I had planned to go home early that evening, but of course, after you've been drinking all day long and now you have a guy that you're interested in, it's a little hard to pull away and just call it a night. At around 9pm, as we usually did, the lines came out, and the real fun started. I asked Tim if it was ok that I had a line or two out of respect. He said he didn't mind at all, and after watching us for a little, he decided it would be ok for him to partake as well. When I asked him if he was ok, he had told me that crack was his problem, not doing the occasional line of coke, which are really one and the same. I didn't think anything of it because, honestly, I didn't really care. When you're high already, you tend not to worry about the feelings of those around you. Now had I been sober and saw him doing lines right after he told me he couldn't, then it may have been a whole different story. But tonight wasn't that kind of night, so I just enjoyed his company and the free drugs I was receiving.

I was a little too loaded to drive home that evening, so Tim offered to drive me back in my car instead. I accepted and at the prospect that there was a chance I was going to get lucky this evening. We ended up talking most of the night, and to my disappointment, even though we made out a little, he wasn't interested in having sex. He just wanted to talk, and I thought to myself, "Who the hell just wants to talk instead of having sex!?" This was new for me because I was usually only interested in one thing. After all, I craved that attention from men and needed that validation that I was enough. To me, sex meant that someone thought I was attractive, and I was capable of being loved, so when Tim told me he wanted to wait, I almost felt a little rejected. Now looking back, I'm pretty sure he was just too high to have sex and wanted to wait until he wasn't going to make a fool of himself.

The next day we had decided to spend the day together. We spent some time at his parent's farm, and then he came back to my place, and I introduced him to my roommates. I don't remember my roommates being all that impressed by Tim, but then again, I wasn't exactly living the wholesome life currently. Things got serious between Tim and I rather quickly, he was spending most nights at my place now, and so we started having the conversation about getting a place together. After getting fired from my last two jobs due to my drug and alcohol use, I finally landed an office job that paid ok, and I worked regular hours again. I figured I was financially stable at this point to entertain the idea of moving out with Tim and being able to support both of us for now. Why on earth I thought this was a good idea is beyond me, but then again, I had learned to become codependent.

Tim had worked on and off throughout that first couple of months of us being together. He worked pouring concrete, which was very seasonal work. Tim got the odd job here and there, but it was never anything long term. One morning Tim called me up and told me he had gotten some work with an old friend of his and that he would start working full time soon. We were both excited because this meant we could move in together officially and not have to worry about money as much. He told me he was going to get an advance so that we could put down a deposit this coming week. He had started work right away, and as Friday approached, I was getting excited to talk about what we needed to buy for our new place. My parents had given me a couch set, which was awesome, but as I slept on a foam mattress currently, we needed to buy an actual bed. I mean, don't get me wrong, it's rather convenient coming home in mid blackout and being able to walk into your room, fall onto the floor, and know you are in bed. Still, I felt it was time for a real bed; after all, I was in my first serious relationship since Tyler, so this was exciting. I waited patiently for Tim to come over that night. He had told me that he was going to get one of the guys to drop him off at my place after he was done working. At 9pm I started to get worried, Tim was already four hours late, and I hadn't heard from him.

This is the part of the story where I should have walked away. But because of my need to be loved and my fear of being alone, I did not. Instead, I waited another two days until I heard from Tim. He didn't sound well and told me he was at his parent's place, and he would call me later. Well, this answer wasn't good enough for me, and so I ended the call, got in my car, and drove over to see him face to face. When Tim came outside, his face looked pale and tired. He kept saying how sorry he was and never called because he got caught up with some old friends. Now had he been telling this to someone who had never gone on a week-long crack bender themselves, then maybe I would have bought it, but I knew the signs from my own use and pushed him over backward out of anger and called him a liar.

Instead of walking away, I took what money I had left and used it to put a down payment on our new basement suite because Tim told me that he would never do this again, and of course, I believed him. I figured that living together would allow me to keep an eye on him and manage our finances together. The first couple weeks were terrific because Tim and I had gotten into such a huge fight the weekend he disappeared that we were in full makeup mode. Of course, this feeling would be short-lived because Tim was an addict, and from experience, once you've had a taste again, it's hard not to go back. You may be wondering how I was managing to keep my shit together and not use during these times, well the truth is I didn't keep it together. Once I realized that Tim was on another bender, I would usually call up a friend and have some similar one of my own. The strange part is that because I knew he was smoking crack, I refrained from using the hard stuff during these absences. I think a sick part of me looked at his use in such a negative way that I actually looked at myself as the better person. Of course, this didn't stop me from doing the occasional line of coke here and there when out with friends because I felt as though it was more classy.

Every time Tim disappeared over the weekend, I seemed surprised for some reason. I didn't want to believe this was going to continue to happen and that one day he would change. Tim would come home, we would fight, then he would spend the rest of the day trying to make up for what he had done. At the end of the evening, I had usually caved in and welcomed him back under the conditions that he never did this again. Other than the emotional abuse I continued to put myself through as a result of staying with Tim, there was no real physical abuse other than my fits of rage when he showed up at home again. I would usually hit him or throw canned goods across the room as I yelled at him for letting me down yet again. Unfortunately, this behavior didn't sit all that well with our neighbors, and not long after, we were asked to leave. I figured that if we got a house a little way out of town, it would be better for Tim because then it wasn't as easy to pick up. I laugh at this now because a drug addict is like a magician. Just when you think it's almost impossible for them to find their next fix, you are blown away with their ability to find anything, anytime and anywhere. I remember having some very crafty ways of my own to get loaded and now looking back at those times if I had just put that much work into my job, relationships, and other areas of my life boy things would have been different, but I wasn't there yet. I was here and not enjoying it all that much.

Tim and I moved again, but this time it was in a beautiful residential neighborhood living in a basement suite under a sweet family. The only downside of this area is that I would have to drive Tim into town often because he still didn't have a vehicle of his own, but we made it work. He managed to stay clean for a couple months, which was a new record, so of course, this added to my belief that he could, in fact, change and that our relationship was actually good for him. Oh, how self-centered was I!? Around this time, he started to have more contact with his son as well. For pretty obvious reasons, he wasn't in a good place with his ex, so up until now, we didn't get to spend a lot of time with his son. This started to slowly change, and we enjoyed the time we got, but Tim's good behavior wouldn't last long with this new responsibility.

I would usually be the one that paid for everything because come payday Tim would disappear for another weekend, and it was often right around the time before we were due to see his son for a few days. We certainly did our best to keep up a good front, but that would eventually grow increasingly difficult. I basically became the sole provider of our household. My pay would go towards taking care of the bills, and I used one of my many credit cards to keep food on the table. One night I had lent Tim a few bucks so he could run out to the grocery store and grab us a few things we needed. I wasn't feeling all that well, so I figured I would trust him to take care of what felt like such a simple task. I laid on the couch and watched the time go by. I just kept wondering, what the hell am I doing??

A few hours later, Tim walked in the door, covered in sweat and clearly shaken up. I was so angry because it was pretty clear he was high. Turns out, Tim had run into town and decided to use the money I gave him to grab a small bag for himself, shocker! Then after that, he went to 7 Eleven and grabbed a few of the items I had asked for on his way home. Apparently, as he pulled out of the parking lot, he had gotten into an accident and hit another car. It didn't sound like his fault, but the problem was that he was high. I had insured his truck a week before for a short time, which given the current situation, didn't sit well. Lucky for Tim, he had a witness that evening, so the police weren't involved at all and had things turned out any different he may not be home at all right now. Regardless I saw red and couldn't think straight. I had stayed in this relationship for much longer than I should have because I believed that I could change Tim. I did things in this relationship that took me to some all-time lows, and that night was one of them.

I grabbed my keys, told him to get in the car, and I drove him to his nearest dealer's place. He looked baffled as I gave him some money to run inside and grab me a bag of crack. He tried to push back on my request, but he could tell by the look on my face that I would not back down. We drove back to our place, and I grabbed one of his pipes, which I had found under the bed a few weeks earlier, and I loaded it up. I sat on the couch directly across from him and lifted the pipe to my lips. Other than the occasional line of cocaine, I hadn't smoked crack in a while, but tonight I wanted to hurt Tim as much as he hurt me. I lit the lighter and inhaled as deep as I could. I held the smoke in for as long as I could and exhaled with a big breath. I had put a fairly big rock on that pipe, and so the high hit me instantly. I hadn't felt this good in a long time, and when I looked over, I saw Tim crying. You see, as messed up as this may sound, although I would still use on occasion, Tim wasn't proud of what he was doing, I don't believe any addict ever is, but he saw me as someone different, someone better. Seeing me smoke in front of him broke his heart. I knew it would affect him to this degree, and that is why I did what I did that night. It was the nastiest thing I could think of other than inflicting bodily harm to him. I continued to take hit after hit from the pipe while he watched, and as I finished up, I knew the rest of the evening would be hell. I didn't have any more money to buy more and coming down from that large of a high wasn't going to be easy, but I wanted Tim to see me suffer because that gave me even more gratification. I finally fell asleep around 6am and slept the whole day away. I felt horrible for what I had done, so I woke up and grabbed a beer to hopefully get rid of this awful headache.

Being as codependent as I was at the time, I was hoping the previous evening events would scare Tim enough so that he would make an effort to get clean. We actually ended up attending a meeting together that evening, and when we left, Tim said he would try to turn his life around once and for all. He asked if I would attend with him on occasion, but I felt as though I was too good for that. After all, doing lines at the bar and drinking was a far cry from being a crack head, right? I mean ok, so I had my problems before, but now I was a little more classy, I thought. Plus, he was the one with the issue, remember, not me. This lasted a couple weeks, and I was starting to gain hope again like I did so many other times. Of course, that hope was crushed again come payday, and I was right back in the place of wondering why on earth I kept doing this to myself. I was so far in debt that I didn't have enough money to cover the rent. We had been late before, but our very kind landlord had warned me that this couldn't keep happening. I was counting on some money from Tim so we could cover the bills this month and not get evicted. Well, that didn't happen because on Sunday, when he came home from his bender, he had nothing left to spare. Looks like we were moving again, the only problem was that this time we didn't really have anywhere to go. For the next couple of weeks, we would camp out in the back of Tim's parent's yard in a tent. You may be asking why the hell wouldn't you go and sleep inside. Well, because Tim would often hide out in his room and get high and the last time I went into his room, there were burnt spoons under the bed and on the floor. I didn't want the reminder, as it made me feel sick to my stomach. I just knew that I had to find us a place soon because this was not a position I thought I would ever be in.

A week later, I ended up finding a basement suite that we could afford. We rounded up enough money for a deposit and moved yet again. We had kept all our furniture in Tim's parent's barn, so at least we weren't coming in with nothing. For the first month, after we moved, Tim had managed to keep himself clean for the most part. We drank together a lot, and what some people don't understand about addiction is that some of us cannot handle anything being put into our system. Myself for example, if I were to smoke a joint today, there is a high probability that it would lead to more. As soon as I have a mind-altering substance enter my system, there is usually only one outcome, more of anything I can get my hands on. Unfortunately, this goes for pain pills and food as well. I'm not limited to just drugs or alcohol, and neither was Tim. Our life seemed to be getting a little better shortly after we moved. Of course, this gave me some more hope. Tim was doing ok and hadn't disappeared since we ended up getting kicked out of our last place, and we had his son regularly as well. I think part of that was because Tim wasn't working as much either. In the industry he worked, it wasn't uncommon to see drug use, and a lot of guys used. Even though we could have used the money, I was super grateful he wasn't in a place where he was tempted. Maybe this time would be different, I thought.

Due to all the stress, I was slowly gaining a lot of weight during this time as well. My drinking had become so heavy that if I estimated correctly over an average weekend, I usually drank around 6000 calories in beer and other beverages. This wasn't including the weekdays or the fast food I would regularly consume. My self-esteem was at an all-time low because I was ashamed about how I was living. Friends were starting to wonder why I kept myself in this situation, and I would play it off as though things weren't that bad. Of course, on the inside, I was being torn apart and hated myself for not having the strength to leave a situation where I was clearly unhappy and heading for a bottom really quickly. I had also contemplated taking my life on several occasions during this time. Tim has started using again, which really was no surprise at this point, but because I had gotten myself to a place where I didn't think I could do better, I continued to put up with this for another 6 months. I had grown attached to Tim's son as well, which didn't help matters any because when things were right, it felt as though I had a family of my own.

The moment I finally woke up was after Tim had started working full time again. It was Friday, and Tim's son was coming over for the weekend. I had assumed that with his son coming over that there was no way that he would disappear. One of the many unfortunate things about addiction though is that once you're loaded, nothing else matters. It's not something that you intentionally do, but it really shows you the power of addiction. I put Tim's son to bed that Friday and sat on the couch crying. It's hard to explain to a 12-year-old why his dad didn't come home to see him. I was heartbroken. Over the next couple of days, I did my best to keep positive and play it off as though Tim had gotten called out of town for work, but it was so painful. On Sunday, I dropped Tim's son off and knew I had to figure out what to do. I couldn't continue to put myself through this emotional pain. Not only that, but the debt I had accumulated had become almost impossible for me to manage with the money I was taking in.

I went home and started to pack some of Tim's belongings up. I called up a friend of mine and told her that I was done. I couldn't handle this anymore, and I had to get my life back. She was super happy to hear this because I think at this point, no one really believed that I would step away from this relationship no matter how much they encouraged me to do so. That afternoon I called Tim's boss and left a message for Tim to come and pick up his stuff after work. About an hour later, Tim called and, of course, like always started to apologize and promised me this would never happen again. This time I didn't believe him and told him that it was too late. He sounded somewhat drunk on the phone, and I could tell this because his anger was coming through when typically, after a weekend bender, he was a little quieter and burnt out. He started to get angry and slammed down the phone. I had a feeling this wasn't the last time I would hear from him this evening. Sure enough, about an hour later, he called again, and this time the tone of his voice started to scare me. He could be an angry person in general, but his anger had never really been taken out on me because he was always the one apologizing. After some more yelling and the threats started, I finally hung up the phone and told him to leave me alone. I was shaken up so I went and took a couple pain killers to calm myself down. I called my mom just so I could forget about what happened, even if only for an hour or so. Once I was composed enough, I decided sleep would probably be the best thing. I locked up the house, took a couple of sleep aids, and decided to try and get some sleep.

As I laid in bed wide awake, I couldn't help but wonder if Tim was going to make his way home that night. I kept replaying what he had said on the phone over in my head, and frankly, it had me worried. About an hour went by, and I still couldn't sleep for some reason. I heard a noise from the street, which sounded like a door slamming. I froze instantly in my bed, praying that it wasn't Tim getting dropped off. I looked over towards the window and saw a shadow walk by. As much as I wanted to get up and grab something to protect myself, the fear I felt didn't allow me to do so. I laid there in my bed paralyzed as I heard the door unlock, and Tim walk in and down the hall. The sounds of his footsteps were so heavy on the floor that I could tell he was full of rage. As he swung open the door and turned on the lights, I looked up at him and begged him to leave. His face was pale, and he was sweating profusely, which was always a sign that he had been using. I knew that I was in trouble. He told me I was not going to leave him and grabbed a glass milk bottle that was full of pennies and threw it towards me. The bottle hit the wall behind me and shattered into tiny pieces all over the floor.

I tried to jump over to the other side of the bed as Tim approached me, but he had grabbed my legs and managed to jump on the bed to pin me down by the shoulders. I tried to push him off me, but I was so tired because of the pills I had taken. I didn't have the strength to get him to let go. I yelled as loud as I could in hopes that the people upstairs would come, or it would at least get Tim to leave out of fear of being caught. He continued to push me into the bed harder as he yelled at me and told me what a bitch I was. I managed to get my leg up, which threw him off balance, and he stumbled to the side of the bed. I tried to slip away, but he grabbed me from my ankles and pulled me as hard as he could off the side of the bed. I tried to stand up, but when I did, he grabbed both of my wrists and slammed me back down on the floor face first. I winced in pain, because not only was he bruising my arms, but now I was laying in the glass that shattered all over the floor. As I continued to scream, this just fueled his anger even more. He started to drag me across the floor and yelled that I wouldn't get away with this. All of a sudden, we both heard a noise coming from upstairs. I continued to scream as loud as I could, and from the first time since this nightmare started, Tim let go and ran out the front door. I laid on the floor sobbing and in complete shock about what had just happened. I couldn't seem to get up, and every part of my body hurt. A few minutes later, I heard the soft voice of my landlord hovering over me, asking me what had happened. I remember looking up at her and saying, "I need help." She helped me up and walked me over to the phone. She told me to call 911 and gave me a wet cloth so I could wipe the blood off my arms and legs. As I waited for the police to arrive, I kept wondering, how did I get here?

I was fortunate that evening. Other than the cuts, bruise and my hurt ego, I never had to see Tim again. I guess when there is enough physical damage from an assault, the victim doesn't always have to go to court and testify unless the defendant pleads not guilty. I was told that after a two-day search, Tim finally turned himself in and seemed very remorseful for his actions. I called up Lara and Kyle and was able to move my stuff out the following day, so I could start to build my life up again, or at least that was the plan in my head. It made me sad to look back at this period of my life. To think that we can put ourselves through this kind of mental abuse for so long because we feel we can't do any better. Years later, I would have to really look at this time in my life, and I realized that even though it wasn't my fault that Tim had attacked me that evening, I had a massive part in enabling the behavior to continue. Because my self-esteem was so low, and my ego kept telling me I wasn't good enough, it kept me in situations that were toxic for me much longer than I would have liked. However, today I have found the tools to work on these parts of myself, and I no longer have to live with these feelings of inadequacy because I know I am loved, and I know I am good enough.

Interestingly enough, the year I got sober, I would actually run into Tim again. Because I hadn't dealt with any of the emotions from this relationship, it was very overwhelming seeing him again. I had walked into a room full of people, and when I looked up, he was directly in front of me. It had been over 10 years since I'd seen him last, and instead of facing him, I turned around and walked away. I hadn't realized that I had never adequately dealt with what happened that night, and so the healing began.

**Lessons Learned:**

* It was not my job to change people. As much as I thought I had this power when I was younger, I had to learn to either accept people for who they are or move on.
* Sticking around in a relationship that was toxic for me enabled the person's behavior that I was with even more. I was basically telling them it was ok to treat me that way when, in fact, it wasn't ok.
* Creating boundaries is a good thing! This was hard for me to learn, but saying no to others is sometimes saying yes ourselves.

**Final Thoughts:**

Have you ever gone through emotional or physical abuse in a relationship and are too ashamed to talk about it? Did you stay in these situations much longer than you would have liked too, or maybe you still are?

Do you want to talk about it? Info@theroadtohealth.me

**Suggested Solution:**

I was trapped in the victim mentality for much longer than I needed to be. Once I sought out help and saw a therapist, the healing began.

Abuse is never ok. Make sure you reach out and ask for help or talk to someone you trust!

## ISOLATION

The first couple of months after the assault was a very dark time for me. I started to experience depression, anxiety, and isolation. I had moved in with Kyle and Lara even though I knew this may not be the best environment for me, given our history together. They were kind enough to let me stay, so I accepted their offer regardless of what the consequences may be. The police were still out looking for Tim and would provide us updates as well as drop by occasionally to see if I was ok. The worst part was that Tim also knew where he could most likely find me, so there was that fear of him showing up. Kyle made sure to always keep an eye out as he wanted to make sure I felt safe. The night before Tim had turned himself in, I remember Kyle bursting into the room where Lara and I were sleeping and telling us to wake up and hide. Both of us jumped out of bed from a dead sleep and started to panic. I think we were all a little on edge those first couple nights. It turned out to be the police letting us know that Tim had just been arrested, and we had nothing to worry about anymore.

There was a sense of relief the day that Tim had turned himself in, but I was not only physically, but mentally and emotionally worn down. This all seemed very surreal, and I wasn't entirely sure how to move forward. I had put myself in a situation where I was so desperate to be loved that I put up with the mental abuse that came along with it for almost 4 years. I had already struggled with my need for approval since I was younger, and now that feeling was just amplified. I didn't understand how someone that apparently said they loved me as often as he did could even think about hurting me the ways Tim did. There is never an excuse for physical abuse to happen in a relationship, and of course, I can now recognize that I wasn't exactly innocent of it. Neither one of us loved ourselves, let alone could love someone else the way they should be.

For the first couple of months, I isolated unless I had to go to work. I was told to go see a therapist to deal with what had happened, but of course, I had no interest in this; after all, I had my own solution. Lucky for me, I found out one of the guys I was working with was dealing coke, so that worked out perfectly. Kyle was also brewing his own beer and wine coolers, so I was able to get alcohol at a super low price and didn't have to go very far to get it. It all worked out perfectly. I knew, however, that I had to be somewhat discreet about my use because when Lara started using heavily again, it didn't go over well with Kyle. Somehow they had managed to stay together even after how bad things had gotten, but I know Kyle was not a big fan of Lara using coke, so this was something I had to keep to myself. I had also gained a bunch of weight, so I knew if I started to use coke again, I wouldn't feel the desire to eat as much because it pretty much got rid of those food cravings. Addiction came in many forms for me. For the most part, it consisted of drugs and alcohol, but as I started to get into my mid 20's food would begin to play a significant role as well, but we'll get into that later.

I had a pretty standard routine going for me over the next couple of months. I would wake up and as hard as it was to do, I would go to work, come home and eat a small meal. I would then go to my room and do a couple lines of coke, grab a few drinks and head out to the living room and hang out with Kyle, Lara, and whomever else was over that evening. It was common for them to have people over every night, so I still felt as though I got in a bit of social time, I was just able to do it from the comfort of my own home. After I got tired of being social and the cloud of weed would start to affect my high, I would retreat to my bedroom, hop on the computer and continue to do lines as I played solitaire all evening and tuned out the rest of the world. Eventually, I would have to try and make sure I could fall asleep, so I would take a couple sleeping pills and smoke a joint to end the evening. It was always difficult to fall asleep, but eventually, I would manage to get in a few hours before having to wake up and do it all over again the following day. This routine took all of the pain and sadness I was experiencing and stuffed it away in a place where I wouldn't have to confront it. I have since learned that when I use this type of solution or strategy to hide my feelings or emotions, they do not, in fact, just go away. They sit there beneath the surface metastasizing until eventually, something would trigger me, and they would all come rushing out in one massive wave. This would only cause me to want to numb the pain even more because I didn't like feelings, they made me feel uncomfortable. For now, though, I was in my safe place, and I had no plans on changing that.

A few months later, my routine of isolation had started to take a toll on me. Besides not wanting to get out of bed because I was just too tired to, I now had no desire to be part of society period. The only sense of normalcy I had was my work, but even that grew increasingly difficult because I just wanted to hide away and not be a part of this world. By now, my roommates started to get a little worried about me. One of our mutual friends was having a birthday party at our favorite pub, and because I hadn't gone out in the last few months, I really did not have any desire to go. I felt as though it would take too much effort, and I wasn't in a functional headspace so why would I think others would want me to show up and bring the rest of the group down. I had dug myself such a big hole of self-pity I no longer saw a way for me to get out of it.

Thank god, my friends were persistent and did not take no for an answer. Until that evening, they hadn't been successful at getting me to leave the house, but for some reason that night, I made a choice to say yes, and today I am so incredibly grateful I did. Reluctantly I got ready to go out and promised myself I would do my best to enjoy the evening. I did a couple of lines before I left just to perk me up, grabbed a few drinks, and headed out. When I got to the pub, I was met with so many friendly faces. It had been months since I'd been out, and even though my head was telling me to go home, there was something in my subconsciousness that was telling me I needed to stay. As the night went on, I enjoyed the excellent company and did some dancing as well. I started to feel better about my decision to come out that night, even though I still wanted to go home and isolate myself in my room. As I stood there talking to a friend, I felt a tap on my shoulder. When I turned around to my surprise, I saw Bev, my best friend from high school, standing in front of me with a big smile on her face. I hadn't seen Bev for several years because we had grown apart about a year after school had ended. Seeing her standing there instantly brought comfort and a sense of familiarity back into my life. I went over to say hello to her family, and she also introduced me to her husband. I couldn't believe what a coincidence it was that the one night I decide to finally go out and be social, I would run into Bev. Remember, back when I mentioned that people come into our lives for a reason? Today I don't believe that this encounter was a coincidence, I think it was fate, and although things didn't exactly change for me overnight, this is when I would experience my first small shift in life. The following Monday, I went to work feeling a little lighter than usual. Things usually felt burdensome and challenging, but for some reason that morning, it was different. I had re-connected with someone that I had respected and admired, and for the first time in months, I did not feel as though I was stuck in that big hole of self-pity. I started to see some hope, and I wanted to hang on to that with every single ounce of strength I had left. I did my best to be as social as I could even though it wasn't much, it was a start. Bev and I had started to email back and forth and had the occasional conversation over the phone, it was great to catch up. Even though we began to share what we had been up to over the last few years, I found it challenging to open up and be completely honest, and this would weigh on me. This is the first time I can remember trying to cover up a part of me that I was so deeply ashamed of. I wasn't ready to expose this side of myself yet because I wasn't finished.

One afternoon I decided it was time to get out and visit some friends. It was a beautiful sunny afternoon. They had a barbecue that day, and I knew that after a few drinks, they would typically bring out the coke, which was just an added bonus. I went into the house to grab another beer and noticed the garage door was open. I heard a couple voices I recognized, so I went in to say hello. Don, the guy I worked with, was there, and in front of him was a big pile of cocaine. They were weighing it out and putting it into flaps for him to sell. I went over and gave him a big hug when he asked, "Do you wanna help out, and I'll make sure your night is taken care of for the evening?" To that, I said, "Fuck ya!" With three of us working away, it didn't take long at all to finish up. Besides, we would just do the occasional line as we worked, which made things so much more enjoyable. It's incredible how such a mundane task can seem so much more enjoyable when you're high. As we wrapped up our work, we went back out into the yard and enjoyed the rest of our afternoon.

We had to make a couple trips to the beer store as well because we were enjoying ourselves so much that the drinks weren't lasting all that long. My intention for that afternoon was to stay for the barbecue and then head home early. I had promised a friend that I would go on a hike the following day, so of course, planning to continue doing what I was doing most likely would result in my bailing as usual. Unfortunately, when drugs or alcohol were concerned, I could have the best intentions in the world to be a good friend, a good daughter, and a good employee. The reality, however, was that when I was loaded, nothing else mattered, and consequences no longer seemed to exist. We carried on all evening, and the more we used, the more paranoid everyone became. Don started to look out the crack in the blinds every so often because he had this idea in his head that cops would find him. At that moment, I remember thinking, Wow, Don has really turned into an addict! Obviously, that was really judgmental coming from me. However, you have to understand that I still didn't really believe I had a problem. I felt that to be labeled as an addict or alcoholic, you needed to be homeless and lose everything. This life I had created only felt normal because of the people I choose to surround myself with at the time. They were doing the same things that I was, so I couldn't see it as an issue. Don was starting to get a little too paranoid, so I decided it was time to head out. I let my friend know and thanked her for a great evening. She asked if I was ok to drive, and of course, as usual, I said yes. As I gathered my things and said my goodbyes, we heard the sounds of sirens. We looked over and saw Don jump towards the window, yelling at us to stay back and hide. We couldn't help but laugh because we knew those sirens weren't for us. A fire truck pulled up to a home just down the street from us and started blocking off the road. More fire trucks and police cars started to show up, blocking off all the streets around us. A couple of us went outside to go see what was going on as Don continued to prepare himself for the apparent invasion he thought he was about to receive.

When we got outside, we noticed it smelled like gas, so we figured that there must be a gas leak in the neighborhood somewhere. Needless to say, I didn't get home until 7am that morning, and as usual, another commitment I had promised to a friend had fallen by the wayside. I carried around a lot of guilt around being as unreliable as I was, but I would always lose control no matter how good my intentions were. I cared deeply about the promises I had given to friends when I was sober. I wasn't a person who got any sort of satisfaction about letting people down. In fact, it ate me up inside. I was powerless over the effects of drugs and alcohol, I just didn't want to admit it. There are times it frustrates me to hear people who don't understand addiction say that we as addicts just need to have some willpower or self-control over our use. Well, I'm here to tell you on behalf of people who suffer it isn't exactly as easy as that. We do, at times, realize what we are doing to others is wrong, and for some of us that make it out of this life alive, we eventually are presented the opportunity to make things right.

A few weeks after my all-nighter, I reached out to Bev and asked if she wanted to meet up on the weekend. I had been asked by a friend to housesit, and so I figured since I didn't exactly enjoy being alone, it would be great to have some good company. Bev and I made plans to go out and do some shopping during the day and then come back and have a movie night. This wasn't the type of weekend I was accustomed to having, but considering the lack of sleep I was getting, I looked at this as a welcomed change. The relationship I had with Bev was a friendship that was healthy for me. I respected Bev a lot, and so it killed me inside trying to hide this whole other life I lived from her. I was scared that if she found out who I really was, she would end our friendship and not want to be associated with someone like me. Bev was aware of what happened with Tim and I, and she knew that I drank a lot because, in high school, it really was no different; it had just progressed over the years and gotten much worse, so I tried to hide what I could in the beginning. Regardless I was really looking forward to that weekend. I really wanted things to change, and having a good influence around did help at times.

On Friday evening, I had plans to go to a house party with Kyle and Lara. My intentions were to stay until around 10pm and then head back to the apartment I was housesitting at and get a good night's sleep so I could be well-rested for the following day. Kyle was keeping an eye on Lara at all times because he knew she had started using again, and with me, in attendance, there was no telling what could happen. The problem wasn't Lara that night, unfortunately. I went downstairs to go hang out with a few friends to enjoy a couple drinks when one of the guests decided to bring out a tray of coke. One of the guys looked over at me and asked, "Hey, Tamar, you in?" For a split second, I felt like saying no. I knew that I had a big day planned tomorrow, and in my mind, there was no way I was going to mess that up. I let everyone else take a turn, so I had more time to make my decision, but every time I heard someone doing a line, it made the desire for me to partake even stronger. I couldn't stand it anymore and so walked over, grabbed the straw, and found the most prominent line I could. When the coke hit my nose, all feelings of guilt went away. My thoughts about what the right thing was in this situation completely vanished. We continued for about an hour when all of a sudden, Lara came to the door. I heard, "What the hell are you doing???" I spun around, and to my surprise, Lara actually looked angry at me. This was not the response I was used to seeing from her, and so I was a little stunned. Kyle walked in soon after, and because he was more worried about Lara going off the rails, he grabbed both of us and said he was taking us home. On the ride home, I got lectured about my behavior, and it felt as though I was in an episode of the twilight zone. The very two people I had used with the most were now upset with me for ruining their evening. I got dropped off at the apartment and did my best to fall asleep that night. Bev wasn't coming over until around

1pm, so I assumed I would be ok in terms of getting enough sleep. Of course, that wasn't the case, and I laid awake for most of the evening well into the morning.

The following day I slept until around noon. I think I may have actually fallen asleep at around 9am, which sucked because I knew it was going to be a struggle to function. When Bev arrived, we went out and did some shopping. It was great to get out of the house because the fresh air managed to keep me awake and alert. You may also be surprised to know that I did not drink coffee during this period of my life. I would take just about any other type of upper, but when it came to coffee, I couldn't stand it. I drank a couple of red bulls and some diet coke, hoping that it would keep me going until after the movie, but those didn't help at all. After dinner, we hung out, and all I remember was trying desperately to keep my eyes open. The consequences of the evening before were hard to hide, and I was struggling to be present. After a short time, Bev decided to go home because I was just too tired to be social. After she left, I went into the bathroom and took a look at myself in the mirror. I had bags under my eyes, and I felt as though I looked sick. At least this is how I perceived myself to look. I started to cry because it was at that moment I knew that if I was going to have good friends like Bev in my life, people who were actually healthy for me, I needed to make some changes. That evening I experienced a desire to change and a small ounce of hope that it may actually be possible.

**Lessons Learned:**

* Isolating myself while being in a state of depression made things so much worse.
* When I started down my destructive path after the assault, I wish I had asked for help right away. I didn't have to suffer in silence all alone.
* I believe that people come into our lives for a reason and when I've chosen to acknowledge what that reason might be, the course of my life changed.

**Final Thoughts:**

It's ok to ask for help when we're struggling. I spent a lot of time suffering in silence when having to deal with feelings and emotions. Then I would get drunk or high to attempt to cover them up. Have you experienced something similar?

Let me know: info@theroadtohealth.me

**Suggested Solution:**

Depression can be very serious if left unchecked. If you know someone who is struggling or you struggle, it's ok to ask for help.

Today when I feel the depression coming on, I make sure to do some meditation as well as exercise. These will usually lessen the impact it has over me.

* Meditation Practice
* Do something active (Walk, Running, Yoga, Gym)
* See Tips & Resources

## CRASH DIETING

I believe it was in late 2002 or early 2003 that I started to become very uncomfortable with my body due to how much weight I had gained over the past few years. It really should not have been a surprise, because when you're drinking upwards of 1000 - 2000 calories in booze per day and eating like crap, it can happen rather quickly. It was the first time I had experienced being overweight to the degree that I wanted to conceal it from everyone. I would wear hoodies or baggy clothes just to disguise the bulge in my stomach. I was about 190 lbs and decided it was time to do something about it. My boss and I had spoken about joining a weight loss program together in the past, but I don't think I had hit a point where it was at the top of mind. After all, I knew that having to watch my calories would entail also having to adjust how much I drank, and I wasn't ready for that. Mind you, I wasn't prepared for that now, but I knew if I didn't do something soon, my weight would get even more out of control and harder to manage.

That afternoon my boss and I went down to Weight Watchers and signed up. I was super excited because after the year I had just experienced, I was ready for some positive changes and a whole new me. We drove over to a meeting on our lunch break and were both super excited to get started. As we did our weigh in, I felt determined, and I think part of the excitement was getting a bunch of free stuff when we registered, because who didn't like free stuff! Looking back, I would have gladly traded all that free stuff that I was so excited about for a simple app to log my food into, but unfortunately, this was back when apps did not exist, so we had to settle for a big ass book to skim through manually. I didn't care, though, because this was the start of a whole new me. I was all in! As an addict, it wasn't just drugs and alcohol I was addicted to. I would overdo EVERYTHING! This included Weight Watchers and every other diet program I would attempt afterward. This behavior does get exhausting after some time; trust me. I'm sure some of you can relate to this feeling. Regardless that day was going to be different. I went home and wrote out all the foods I could think of that I could afford and keep my points down. I went out and did my shopping right away and started to track everything I ate. I even decided to get in some exercise, which I hadn't done a lot since I stopped playing sports after high school. I would start with walking, followed by running for a very short time and when I say a short time I mean about two days. After that attempt, I went back to walking just to be safe.

During the first month, I lost about 10 lbs or so. You would think this would make anyone on a weight loss journey super happy, but not me. I needed the weight to fall off quicker because I was starting to become miserable at the fact I couldn't drink as much as I usually did. If I wanted to eat well and eat enough, I didn't have a lot of points left over to drink a lot of beer. I knew there had a be a better way, and so after my next weigh-in, I went home and started to create a plan. For those of you that have tried Weight Watchers before and found success using the program, you know that it's a great system to lose weight. That is unless you are me, and you can figure out how to manipulate just about everything. I could manage to turn anything healthy into something not so healthy if I put my mind to it, and this program was no different. For those of you not aware, Weight Watchers back then was on a points system. Depending on how much you weighed, you would get a specific amount of points per day. You could eat pretty much anything you wanted, too, as long as you didn't go over your designated daily points. The other benefit was that if you got in some exercise, you would receive additional points to eat a little more! Let me tell you when I found out I could drink an extra three beers just for walking an hour per day all of a sudden that hour walk didn't seem all that bad anymore. I even remember walking in the rain at times because dammit I was getting those extra drinks! Remember, I was all in, and this was just a sacrifice I had to make.

When I got home, I took out my book and started to figure

out what foods would fill me up with the least amount of points. I also went through my past food journals and wrote down anything I had eaten in the past with a low count of points. I was so desperate to hit my goal so that I could jump straight back into my old lifestyle, but with a whole new look. I was willing to sacrifice variety in what I ate because boring seemed to be the answer. After about an hour, I finally came up with a plan that would allow me to stick to my 31 points per day, and this did not include my hour walk, which made it 37! Now before I disclose the measures, I went to, and the plan I followed, I want to state that this should not be followed or attempted if you are a responsible adult. I would start my day off with a bag of microwave popcorn, which was ideal because it was worth only one point. I would then have a diet coke to drink so that I got a little flavor in my day, followed by another bag of popcorn for lunch. There was the odd time I would indulge and go out for lunch with a co-worker, but that wasn't often in the beginning. When I got home from work, I would make sure to get out for a walk, which provided an additional six points making my allowable total 37 for the day. I would then make one veggie burger patty and count out seven oven-baked french fries. If I felt like sacrificing a couple of beers, I would add a little mayo for my fries. This plan allowed me the luxury of drinking anywhere between 8 - 18 drinks per evening. Back then, you could also bank any unused points as long as you used them that week. I would often bank a few points here and there so I could drink more on the weekends. This strategy made it easier not to have to track how many drinks I had on the weekends, which was always a challenge when it came to a night out with friends.

My plan was working rather well until about a month later, when I started to experience the dreaded plateau. I was getting frustrated because, of course, even though I was able to drink again, my food choices were very restricted, and it was becoming increasingly difficult to maintain, not to mention boring as hell. I decided to kick it up a notch.

I went into a supplement store and started to look around at all the diet pills available. I walked up to the cashier and asked for the most potent pills they had. She walked me over to one of the shelves and showed me a bottle she recommended. I almost went into shock when I saw the price of the pills, but I felt as though this was an emergency, and it would be money well spent. The cashier asked me if I had experience with diet pills before, and of course, I lied and said yes. I wasn't open to receiving a recommendation that I should start with something a little milder. I was on a mission to reach my goal weight and resume life without the added stress of counting my food daily. I didn't look at this as a lifestyle change instead of more of a temporary detour to help me get to my destination as quickly as possible. The sad part is that this program was probably one of the easiest I could have adapted as a new lifestyle because it wasn't restricting me to specific types of food, I had done that all on my own. Excited about my purchase, I ran home to read all the instructions front to back. I wanted to make sure that I knew precisely the maximum dose I could take safely because I was sure as hell not taking the minimum dose. The bottle said to take with food, and because I had already eaten and it was too close to bedtime, I decided to start taking it first thing in the morning.

The following day I went off to work excited and with only one thing on my mind. How quickly were these pills going to work? I grabbed a bag of popcorn, cracked open a can of diet coke, and popped the first few pills. I'm not exactly sure what I expected after taking them, but in my mind, I thought I would experience some additional energy. I can tell you this was not at all what I experienced. I first started to sweat like crazy, which made me eat another bag of popcorn because I assumed I was feeling jittery from my low caloric intake. I also grabbed another diet coke because maybe the taste would take my mind off the fact that I felt utterly sketched out. My heart was beating so fast in my chest that I felt as though I was about to have a heart attack. The bottle told me to take another few around lunchtime, which I was slightly concerned about now. I'm glad I sat in a cubical where no one could see me unless they came around to discuss something specifically. I would go back and forth from the bathroom to wipe the sweat off my face. I was super grateful had I brought a hoodie with me that day as well, so people couldn't see the fact I was sweating right through my t-shirt as though I had just run a marathon. I was grateful that my job required me to go out into the shop on occasion because the shop was cool and it would allow me a little time to get some fresh air. I had managed to make it through that entire first day, even after taking the second dose. I will admit I had trouble sleeping that evening even though the bottle said that as long as I take the last dose before 2 pm, I should be ok. That was not the case for myself; instead, I laid in bed with my eyes fully open, thinking that this better be worth it. You would think that after a day of feeling as though you were on the worst high imaginable one would stop taking these pills, but as I mentioned before, I was on a mission, and I would do what it took even if I had to suffer a little as a result. I continued to take them daily, even when I felt sick and dizzy. I would make sure to go on long walks after work to dispurse some of the pent-up energy, but that didn't help all that much either. The only thing that provided some relief in the evening was the case of beer. I drank to slow down the jitters. The smart thing to do would have been to just stop taking the pills, but you have to remember back then I hadn't developed a healthy mindset around food or a healthy relationship with it. I only wanted to lose weight and nothing more. This would be my first weight loss journey after all, so I wasn't yet aware that I would continue to struggle to keep the weight off time after time if I didn't change my way of thinking. That would come much later!

A couple of months later, I knew I was close to my goal weight, and I was super excited to go to the meeting and find out. As I waited in line, the anticipation was killing me. When it was my turn to jump on the scale, I put my card down on the desk and stepped up to see just how much all my hard work had paid off. I looked up at the woman behind the counter, and a big smile came across her face. She looked down at my card, and there she wrote my goal weight and gave me a big gold star sticker. She said, "Congratulations, Tamar! You did it, and now it's time to start the maintenance part of the program." I'm pretty sure she said more than just this, but I was just too excited that I had reached my goal I kind of blocked the rest of the conversation out. I sat through the meeting even though all I could think about was going out that night and celebrating with a few drinks and a delicious meal. I was also going to throw away the diet pills I had been taking and buy a few new shirts as I had sweat stains on most of my old ones. I had finally arrived, and this nightmare they called a diet was over. After I reached my goal, I called up a friend and went out for a bite to eat. I had a few beers and enjoyed a big delicious burger and fries. For the first time in months, I didn't have to count out seven oven fries; instead, I could enjoy the real deep-fried ones. Going home that night, I didn't feel all that well, but I didn't care because I was satisfied. I had been depriving myself for so long that I was willing to suffer the consequences of overeating. I tried to continue my daily walks for a time after I hit had my goal, but of course, this now felt like work, and all I wanted to do was relax. My willpower had run out.

Now I realize that my example was a bit extreme, and I could have even caused myself some severe health problems as a result of my actions, but it wouldn't surprise me if others have done the same if not worse. It's no wonder so many people struggle with weight loss today. We put ourselves through torture for a while so that we can have the body we think we so desperately desire. After we reach that goal, we are so exhausted from the amount of willpower and energy required that we just give up and try again later. After this experience, I tried Weight Watchers a few more times, but with no success. It wasn't because the program that didn't work, it was because I chose not to develop the right mindset. The unfortunate part is that I would continue to put my body through this torture for years to come and continually seek out quick fixes to my weight problems. It was where I laid the foundation of what it meant for me to be on a diet, and as I look back at this time, I wish that someone had taught me about mindset above all things and then how to develop a more healthy relationship with food itself. That was something I would have to learn much later in life.

Lessons Learned:

* When I created a healthy mindset around weight loss, it doesn't take as much willpower to be consistent.
* My weight loss journey did not have to be painful. I learned that I could customize it, so it met my own personal needs.
* When I would lose weight by doing something drastic, the weight never stayed off very long.
* I had to learn to give myself grace when things didn't go as planned and realize it was ok to make mistakes.
* I became more open-minded when it came to my health journey. It felt good to try out several different methods and strategies until I found the one's that worked for me and my body type.
* I only had to use my willpower early on, and then eventually, I developed a new habit.

Final Thoughts:

Have you ever gone to any length to lose weight so you could stop feeling that body shame?

Tell me about it! Info@theroadtohealth.me

**Suggested Solution:**

Habits have been a big part of my success. If you have a goal in mind, start to develop small habits you can do throughout the week that will bring you one step closer to that goal. Over time this will lead to consistency and progress.

* See Tips & Resources

## FINDING LOVE

The first time I felt as though I experienced true love was when I met my first husband, Gary. We worked together and sometimes would bump into each other in the lunchroom. One of those encounters he started to ask me some questions in regards to the amount of weight I had lost and what I was doing to stay active. At the time, Bev and I would meet up in Vancouver and go rollerblading along the waterfront and then go grab a bite to eat after. This became one of my favorite ways to spend an evening, plus it was keeping me in shape and out of trouble for the most part. Gary's eyes lit up, and he told me he had a pair of rollerblades and would love to join me one evening if I was up for some company. I was slightly hesitant because Gary had a reputation at our work for being a bit of an asshole to those he worked with. I will tell you that he did take his job very seriously, he was damn good at it, but his downside was that anyone who didn't work as he did was considered an idiot in his eyes. Hence why he got the reputation he did, so I wasn't all that sure how he and I would get along. In any event, I thought I would take a chance and say yes, and so we decided to meet up the following afternoon at our local shopping center after the stores closed, so we had the whole parking lot to practice on. Gary had mentioned that it had been years since he went rollerblading last, so he wanted a bit of a refresher before Bev and I took him out to the big city. Although we had a lot of fun that evening and laughed a lot, Gary wasn't all that good and actually looked as though he had never rollerbladed in his life. It was a fun evening, and as I got to know Gary, even though his rollerblading wasn't all that good, I was really enjoying his company. He gave me a ride home after we finished up, and as I opened the door to get out, he asked if I would like to go on a date with him that weekend. Of course, I said yes and that I looked forward to it.

On our first date, Gary showed up looking and smelling amazing. This was such a change from the guy I was used to seeing at work. I think my heart actually skipped a beat as he gave me a hug to greet me. If I remember right, he even had some flowers with him. He ended up taking me back to his place and made me the most fantastic dinner I think that I've had in my entire life. Gary was a great cook and probably should have used those skills to become a chef, although, with this work ethic, he would have been one of those angry animated chefs you see on TV. Regardless he put so much attention and detail into the evening and somehow I already knew I would marry this man. For the next couple of weeks, we started to hang out a lot. I would spend the night at his place, and because he was working evenings, it gave me a chance to have some alone time until he came home. Part of the reason why I was staying over at Gary's as well was that at the time, I was still living with Kyle and Lara and Lara had started using a lot again. I hadn't used any hard drugs since the evening I got in trouble at that house party because I was determined to turn my life around. I knew that if I wasn't careful, all it would take was one evening out with Lara and a few drinks before I was doing coke again. I was doing a pretty good job at keeping myself out of trouble, and I was hoping it would stay that way. I had told Gary what was happening at home, and he was aware of my history. Gary urged me to keep that stuff out of our relationship due to his own struggles with substance abuse. Staying clean back then wasn't as easy as I thought it would be. Each and every time I drank, the cravings would get triggered, but the difference this time is I was surrounding myself with people who didn't use, so I wasn't exposed to it as much. This could all change in a heartbeat, and I was very aware of it. Gary asked me a couple weeks after we started dating to move in with him. It made sense since I was staying over most nights anyways. Lara and I had become very close during the years we used together. We had gone through a lot of good and bad times and had so much history. It was incredibly hard to walk away from that. Even though I loved Lara, I knew I had to distance myself from our friendship because she was starting to get to a terrible place in her own addiction. After I moved in with Gary, I wouldn't see Lara again for a few years, but as with a few people in my story, we would eventually cross paths again and share our stories of recovery.

Moving in with Gary felt terrific those first few months. He would cook me dinner, and we would often enjoy a bottle of wine and some captain Morgan's spiced rum afterward. I felt as though I had a perfect life. Although Gary was pretty adamant about not using harder drugs, the fact that I was with someone that enjoyed drinking as much as I did ended up working out perfectly. Almost everything we did together involved alcohol, to be honest. We would go to the movies and grab a small bottle of rum so that we could add it to our diet coke. Usually, after the movie was done, we would head down to the pub and play some pool together. When the weather was beautiful, we would pack up some chairs, towels, a cooler full of drinks and snacks, and hang out at the beach or lake all day long. I started to introduce Gary to all my friends, and they really liked him as well, which made me super happy because my last relationship almost cost me some of those friendships. Gary was the kind of guy that loved to have people over for dinner, drinks, and games night. He was passionate about what he cooked and always did his best to give our guests the best experience in terms of food and fun. We even joined a softball team together, which all gave us even more of an excuse to hang out. It felt as though my life was complete and perfect now.

I had never quite recovered from the debt I got myself into while I was with Tim. I had maxed out all four of my credit cards, had a student loan and a line of credit. I had an old car that I didn't trust to go very far in case it broke down, so I started the feel the pressure of living paycheque to paycheque. I had dug myself a hole of debt that I felt I couldn't get out of. Living with Gary helped a little, but my payments became more significant than what I got paid. Regardless I knew I had to start getting out of debt, so I went to seek out credit counseling. I was embarrassed to do so because I knew it would affect my credit, and it had taken me so long to build it up in the first place. Little did I know that this wouldn't be the first time this happened in my life, and it would just get worse, but we'll talk about that a little later. You see, I'm the type of person who will usually try something twice even if it goes seriously wrong the first time around. I do eventually start to learn from my errors, but I'm the touch the stove twice, even if it's a hot one, kind of girl. At the time, I felt as though I was doing all the right things. I had an amazing boyfriend, great friends, a good job, and my social life was great. Gary and I still worked together back then until one day, something had happened between him and his boss. He came storming into the office and told me he'd meet me at home.

Shortly after, my boss came and spoke with me about what happened just to make sure I didn't get upset. I defended Gary because I knew he was an excellent worker; he only had a bit of a temper when it came to working with people he didn't agree with. I went home a few hours later, and when I got there, Gary was so wasted he could barely walk. Not only was he a hot head at times, but his emotions would often drive him to the bottle. This was the first time I started to recognize that just like I did, he drank his feelings away. I tried to console him, but instead, I jumped right in and joined him.

He found a new job fairly quickly because he was great at what he did. His new job would entail that he worked four ten-hour shifts, Monday through Thursday. He loved this idea because it gave him a three day weekend. I gotta be honest, I was a little jealous. He started to make some friends at his new job, which was great because he was usually a loner. I was happy for him because I think he really needed this change. On Fridays, he would go out with his new work buddies, and I was ok with that until he showed up one afternoon to pick me up from work, and he was utterly wasted. Apparently, he had gone golfing for the day and then had more than a few drinks at the clubhouse. I wasn't angry at him for being drunk, but when I got into the car, he could barely keep his eyes open and was hunched over the steering wheel because he drank so much. Writing this actually makes me cringe because I was no better. I made him let me drive us home so he could go and pass out to sleep off his hangover. Anytime he went out after this, he would promise he wouldn't drive in that condition again. Well, that was easier said than done. I had some big-time trust issues because of my relationship with Tim, so when it came to Gary lying to me, I never took it well. You could say I was a little unstable at times. When Gary would go out with his work friends, I always feared he would come home wasted. It seems funny to me now because we were one and the same. So basically, it was ok that he drove drunk with me in the car, but it was not ok for him to do it on his own. Starting to see some more codependence creep up here, but I wouldn't fully understand what that meant until much later.

One evening Gary came home and let me know there was a position opening up at his work that I should apply for. It was more money than I was making now, and we could always drive in together, which made things easier. I started to wonder if it was a good idea to work together again. I believe some people would actually put some thought into this decision, right? Then there is me; I have control issues, and when I feel as though things are out of control, my world crumbles down around me. So I applied for the job right away! To my surprise, I was notified only a couple days later that I got the job, and I was super thrilled about it. I gave my notice at my current job, and although I was sad to leave the friends I worked with, I felt it was time for something new. I would make new friends, and now instead of just Gary going out on Fridays and getting wasted with co-workers, I could join them as well. We had worked together in the past, so it wasn't all that strange working with Gary again.

Like before, Gary was out in the shop, and I was in the office, so we didn't see each other. The company we worked for actually had a lot of couples that worked together, so we fit right in. On the weekends, we would host poker nights and often go out to the pub together. It felt as though we were part of a family, and I really enjoyed that feeling because it made me feel like I belonged. My life was complete once again! I wouldn't notice it at the time, but there was a pattern developing in my life. Each time there was a change of scenery, the new friends I would attract were people precisely like Gary and myself. I've heard it said that you are like the five people you hang out with the most, and today I genuinely agree with this statement. However, even though I always leaned towards hanging out with people who partied a lot, I did have some very stable friendships as well. I am fortunate a few of these friends stuck by me even after they would watch me screw things up over and over again. Unfortunately, these were the friends that I would often bail on if drinking plans came up even though I hadn't planned on it. We don't often see what we're doing to people when we're stuck in this type of lifestyle, and it's unfortunate. I have also since made amends to these people, and today they are my biggest cheerleaders and gave me so much strength as I learned to turn my life around. Back then, I was only interested in having a good time and getting wasted, and for the rest, nothing else mattered.

About a year and a half into our relationship Gary told me he wanted to take me away for the weekend. A friend of mine called me a short time after and hinted that the reason Gary wanted to take me away might be because he was going to propose. After a little persuading on my end, it wasn't hard to get my friend to crack. She burst out with excitement and told me all about the ring and was ecstatic about the idea of us getting married. Gary and I were having some problems in our relationship at that time, and I assumed that by getting married, it would fix everything. I had trust issues, which, of course, had developed over the years from other relationships. I really believed getting married was the answer. Somehow I thought that having a ring on my finger would ease the jealousy and lack of trust I was feeling. The ring was the key! I would no longer be this insecure little girl. Instead, I would transition into a strong, confident woman. Well, it didn't exactly happen like that, but I was a dreamer, and so I would roll with it for now. I was really excited about the next chapter of my life. I mean, isn't getting married the right thing to do?!

After about eight hours and multiple ferries, we finally arrived at our destination. It was a little island located off Vancouver Island, and it was beautiful. The island's population was tiny, but it was full of fun-loving hippy types. Our campsite was surrounded by a beautiful beach, a market where we could buy all our food and some very kind people. Even though we had hundreds of dollars worth of booze on us, we were also pleasantly surprised they had a little beer store on the island. So for the next seven days, we ate and drank to our heart's content. Could life get any better than this? All of a sudden, everything that troubled me in regards to our relationship had vanished, and I was preparing myself to say yes to the man I truly loved. Yup, we were going to be together forever.

I can't remember which day it happened because, of course, when you're only drinking, eating, and playing cards all week, things become a bit of a blur, but one evening Gary told me to dress up as nice as I could. We had just spent some money we didn't have on a beautiful painting of a restaurant that he was about to take me to. This place overlooked the beach, and the night couldn't have been more perfect. The weather hadn't been great the entire week we were on the island, but this evening was a beautiful sunny day. Upon arriving at the restaurant, I couldn't believe the view, it was gorgeous. Gary had gotten us a table near the waterfront, and we ordered a bottle of wine to share. After the server poured our glasses, Gary made a toast to a wonderful week away. Right after that, he pulled out the ring and said, "Tamar, will you marry me?" I did what any super surprised woman would do that already knew this was coming and mustered up the best look of shock and surprise I could and said, "Yes, of course, I will marry you!!" To make it even better, I would continue to talk about how surprised I was and how I had no idea this was coming. It felt like the right thing to do because clearly, Gary had this all very well planned out. The painting we bought that we couldn't afford would always serve as a memory of this evening. The rest of the week was terrific, and I felt as though we were newly dating again. Our relationship felt revitalized because I just knew married life was going to change us! It was going to make us stronger and fix all our problems because surely I wouldn't get insecure with a ring on my finger, right? Oh, how naive I was. I would learn a short time after the wedding that even our parents knew that getting married was a bad idea. It would have been nice to have been told this before the wedding, but then again, I probably wouldn't have listened anyway.

Gary and I got married at a friend's home with a large field located behind their yard, which we used for people who wanted to camp. It worked out really perfectly for those who didn't want to drive or take a cab home. We decided to go with a simple Hawaiian themed wedding because neither Gary nor I were fancy people. My best friend Bev was my maid of honor, and Gary had his Dad as his best man. I had family from Holland fly out, which made the day even more special. My Oma was there (grandma for those of you that do not know the term), and my aunt and two cousins also came out. I made sure to have a couple drinks before we got started because my nerves were unsettled. I loved Gary a lot, and even though our relationship wasn't a terrible one, we were having a rough time then, so a few drinks would help give me the comfort I needed. As I walked down the aisle, I could see the love in his eyes. I know Gary really cared about me, and today I still don't regret having him in my life. He did his best to take care of me and make sure my needs were met. The unfortunate part was that both of us relied on alcohol to deal with our problems, so when emotions surfaced, it was never pretty. Needless to say, our wedding day turned out perfect. All of our guests enjoyed themselves, and we went on late into the night. Apparently, I was told after the fact that when my boss left, I was doing a keg stand. Don't worry though I was told I had removed my wedding dress, so I kept it somewhat classy.

I was hugely hungover the next morning, and it was a bit of a struggle to help with the cleaning. We got through fairly quickly and then headed home to open gifts and pack up for our honeymoon. Gary and I decided instead of going somewhere tropical, we would head down to Los Angeles for four days and then drive up to Las Vegas for the last few days before heading home. The morning we left, I woke up with an incredibly sore throat. It felt as though I was swallowing glass, and I had a feeling I was coming down with strep throat because I had gotten it many times before. There wasn't time to go see a doctor before we got our flight, so I was just going to have to put up with it. At least I had been diagnosed with gallstones a few weeks before the wedding, so I had a large container of painkillers I could just take with me to ease the pain for both. Even though I'd love to tell you the exact details of our honeymoon, I don't remember all of it. I do remember most of our first stretch in Los Angeles. We rented a car and spent some time in Disneyland, driving up the coast and trying out restaurants we had seen on TV. We even hit up a Dodgers game for some fun. We always had a bag of drinks with us in the car so we could crank the tunes and enjoy the ride. After the fourth day, we packed up all our things and drove up to Las Vegas. I had been to Las Vegas before, and typically it ended up being a shit show, and this time was no different. We started our morning by the pool and walked up and down the strip with drinks in our hands. We got smart and picked up a large bottle of vodka, so we didn't always have to buy drinks, the rest of our time there was a blur. I would wake up most mornings, not knowing how we managed to get back to the hotel the night before. Usually, I had a large drink by the side of the bed that I don't remember purchasing. You know the ones that come in a tube that you actually need a strap around your neck to hold? I was popping the painkillers like crazy because my throat felt like it was bleeding, and my gallstone attacks were beginning to happen more frequently. After we got home, I had to go see the doctor and was told that I would need to spend the next week at home until my strep throat cleared up. I was ok with that due to the fact my hangover was so bad that being able to have some drinks at home would make things more bearable.

I always imagined that Gary and I would make the perfect couple, and for a while, I truly believed we were. Not long after our wedding, I would realize that marriage really didn't change anything. At the end of the day, we were two alcoholics that didn't want to deal with our problems. When things are already going wrong, and there is a lack of trust in a relationship, marriage certainly didn't make things better. I also voiced at various points in our relationship that I wanted to have kids, which didn't happen either. When we first met, he agreed to it, but then as time went by, I believe our lifestyle played a roll in his decision to not have children. I also managed to convince myself that there was no way I could go for nine months without having a drink anyway, so who was I to have kids. I assumed that I had gained acceptance on these types of issues and was moving on when, in fact, my resentments would only start to build because they were left unresolved.

**Lessons Learned:**

* Keg stands are apparently not considered classy for women on their wedding night, but I sure rocked it!
* Marriage did not fix all my problems.
* If I wanted to remember my entire honeymoon, I probably shouldn't have gone to Vegas.
* When two alcoholics get married, it can make for a very challenging marriage and mask a whole bunch of underlying problems.
* I had to learn how to love myself before I could truly love someone else. Even though I cared about and loved my husband, I still hadn't dealt with my own issues.

**Final Thoughts:**

Have you ever found yourself committing to something because you felt as though it was the right thing to do? Then, later on, you realized it wasn't?

I'd love to hear about it. Info@theroadtohealth.me

**Suggested Solution:**

Today when I have to make a big decision, and I'm not sure of the answer, I will usually sleep on it. This pause allows me the time to process what I may or may not be getting myself into. If I wake up unsure, then I know it's not the right choice now. I will also run ideas by someone I trust that will give me their honest feedback. This strategy has gotten me out of making some pretty bad choices!

* See Tips & Resources

## BAD DECISIONS

A few months after our wedding, I finally had the surgery to have my gallbladder removed. I was a little excited because it was the first time I would have surgery, and I knew that meant pain killers afterward. I hadn't used drugs for a while, and this was the closest thing without actually breaking the rules Gary had laid out before we got married. The surgery went well, and because Gary had to work that day, my friend Stacy came to pick me up. She brought me a cheeseburger just like I had asked and brought me home after stopping by the pharmacy. To my surprise, I received a large bottle of pills which I knew Gary would not let me keep. As soon as I got home, even though I was partially out of it, I was smart enough to know that if I didn't remove some of the pills and stash them away, I would be forced to throw a good portion of them out. Like I had assumed, Gary was a little surprised with how much they had given me and so he told me to be careful with how much I took.

The next couple of days were great! Gary was working, and I had some time off to recover, so I was able to double up on my dose without him knowing. By the third day, I started to get a little bored and antsy. I wasn't used to spending time by myself, and even though I was enjoying it, for the most part, I felt no pain due to the pills and thought it wouldn't be a terrible idea to go out. I called up my friend Stacy, and she offered to come and pick me up so I could come out to her and her husband's place for a few drinks. Now just to give you a little history before we go any further, my friend Stacy and I had an extremely codependent friendship. I'm not going to say she wasn't a good friend because she was and would do anything for me. But our friendship wasn't always super healthy, and I played a significant role in all of this. We drank almost every time we hung out together, and most evenings turned into a lot of unnecessary drama. There were many times Gary and I would have plans with friends in the evening, and if we made a stopover at Stacy and her husband's place on the way out, we more often than not canceled our original evening plans. This got so bad that one weekend I was supposed to attend a close friend's bridal shower and never showed up because I was too drunk. The worst part of this was that only a few weeks later, I did the same thing on the night of that same friend's bachelorette party. I always had good intentions but fell short often. There were times I started to think that our friendship was harmful, but after those first few drinks, I would forget somehow.

Stacy was always the first one I called when shit hit the fan in my relationship with Gary, and our solution would be to go out and get drunk. This was an arrangement I was ok with. So a few days after the surgery, I called Stacy up, and she came right over to pick me up. We stopped by the liquor store to grab some beer and went back to her place. Her husband was home as well, so the three of us enjoyed a few drinks and lunch together. I made sure to text Gary and let him know I would be home by dinner and that I was being taken good care of. I skipped out the part that I was having a few drinks because as long as I made it home on time, he wouldn't have to know. Gary didn't trust my friendship with Stacy, and he had every right not to. I had made sure to bring a couple extra pills with me that afternoon just in case. I was still recovering and had to watch that I didn't pop my stitches. We were enjoying the afternoon so much, so I decided to stay for dinner. I called Gary and let him know that I would be home a little later. He sounded a bit concerned on the phone because he was very aware of how my evenings with Stacy usually turned out. After convincing him I wouldn't be late, we carried on. That night we continued to drink all evening, and the last thing I remember is Stacy telling her husband she was going to drive me home and her whispering to me that we were going to stop by the pub on the way for a nightcap. I'm not sure what pub we ended up at, but the next thing I remember, I was lying in bed covered in my own vomit, with Gary standing over me yelling. I had no idea how I got home, and when I tried to sit up, I felt a sharp pain in my stomach. My stitches had broken, and I had forgotten to take my pain pills, so the numbness had worn off. My head was pounding, and I assumed Gary was angry at me because I had gotten sick in bed and didn't even realize I was doing it. I'm grateful he was kind enough to turn me onto my side, so I didn't choke to death. Gary was a bit of a clean freak and didn't take too kindly when I got sick after a night out. I guess he was also probably a little mad that I was supposed to stay home and recover but decided it was fine to venture out for a quick visit with a friend. Again, good intentions, but I often failed to keep up with the action part of those intentions.

Stacy had been a friend who was in and out of my life because things would often get out of hand when we hung out. I remember one evening we went to a concert together and we were down on the floor close to the stage. We had agreed that if we lost each other during the evening, we would meet up at the end of the concert in a designated spot. Stacy was the type of person that quickly attracted men and always got into trouble. She also seemed to have a point of no return that if she drank too much, once that switch would flip, she became very unreasonable. It was a bit of a crapshoot to know what was going to happen next, but it usually wasn't something positive. That is just what happened the night of the concert. She wanted to go right up to the front and ended up being pulled over the divider and invited backstage. I waited after the show for over an hour at our meeting spot, and she never showed. This wasn't abnormal behavior, and for some reason, I continued to put up with it for a long time. Often times after these types of things happened, Stacy would make up for it in other ways, and of course, I was quick to forgive, a pattern I developed a long time ago. I had no boundaries yet and didn't understand the meaning of codependence at all. I would later realize that part of the reason I allowed a lot of these relationships to continue was due to my strong desire to be loved and needed. As unhealthy as our friendship was, Stacy made me feel loved, and no matter how bad things got between us, I always forgave her.

Before I started to write this book, I had laid out areas of my life I wanted to talk about. My objective was to be as vulnerable as possible because I was tired of letting shame rule my life anymore. In fact, a lot of these memories came flooding back as I wrote the first draft. There are things in this book that I have never told people until now. There is a sense of freedom I got from writing it all down, and this story is no different.

Towards the end of my time spend with Stacy, we would often have couples weekends. Our goal for the weekend was to eat good food and get as drunk as possible. We would often play games all evening, and then at some point, the switches flipped. Stacy would become unmanageable, and I would near blackout. Stacy would often get super pissed at her husband over god knows what. We were used to this happening, so it never came as a shock. They made up, and we would carry on with our night. A few times, we started to play truth or dare, and there would be naked streaking from the guys and some making out between Stacy and I. The guys loved this, so it started to become something that happened a little more often.

Things were starting to change at that point in our friendship. There were evenings that Stacy and I would hang out and get wasted then end up making out back at her place or mine. Nothing ever happened beyond that as far as I can remember, but I remember feeling confused the next day. Part of me felt ashamed because I was doing this right in front of my husband, and it almost felt as though I was cheating on him even though most of the time, he was aware of it. One of those nights, I stopped what was happening, and Stacy got really offended. I told her I was going to head off to bed, and she could crash on our couch. Stacy was in one of her blackouts and strongly objected to staying now. I told her she wasn't going to drive home, and so I grabbed her keys and walked away. Stacy followed in anger and tried to grab the keys while I blocked her from leaving. She started to hit my chest and yell at me until she finally gave up and went back over to the couch. She passed out almost instantly, and I went to bed but didn't have a good feeling about things after that. I needed a change because I felt as though our friendship had hit a new level that I wasn't ready to explore. I don't blame Stacy for what happened in our friendship. We both drank a lot, and as I said, once that blackout came on, we were never sure what was going to happen. We had a lot of good times, but more often than not, when alcohol was involved, it wasn't healthy.

That first year of marriage, Gary and I decided it was time to move. Things were getting out of hand with Stacy, and the city we lived in brought with it a lot of temptation. I had spent a lot of my time there in my addiction, so it held a lot of bad memories. After a short discussion, we both agreed it would probably be better for our relationship if we moved and started over somewhere else. We checked out a few listings and found a place to go look at that afternoon. When we arrived, the landlord was great, and the condo was on the fourth floor with a small deck overlooking the courtyard. It was spacious and relatively new, which was much better than our current place. The best part is that it was currently empty so we could move in right away. We filled out the paperwork on the spot and decided to go visit some friends in the area to start celebrating. It wasn't too long after that the landlord called us back and accepted our application.

Gary and I were both super excited because it felt like a fresh start. Things were starting to get tense in our marriage because of my friendship with Stacy, and I thought it would be better to live a little further away. Stacy and I still kept in touch, but we didn't see each other all that much after we moved. One evening Stacy and her husband came out for a visit, and after a few drinks, we decided we would head over to a friend's house party. Things started to get weird after Stacy had too much to drink. She wasn't happy with my new friendships, and I felt as though she was jealous. I know my other friends started to feel this as well and asked me what was going on. I got embarrassed easily, so I played it off like there was something wrong with her, which looking back now, I realize that I had a much more significant role in all of this than I thought. We ended up back at our place, fighting in the underground garage. I told her she was being unreasonable and that I had other friends, so she needed to deal with that. We hung out so much we had become dependent on each other. I would often bail on my other friends, so it was no wonder why this change came as a surprise to Stacy. She yelled back, saying, "I thought I meant more to you than just a friend!" Stacy was pretty drunk that evening, so I wasn't sure if it was her talking or the alcohol. It was often hard to tell to be honest. We didn't hang out for a few months after this because I felt as though things were just getting too weird, and I didn't want to go any further down this path.

Gary and I started to settle into our new home and enjoyed the company of our work friends. There was a lot less drama to start off with, but that would soon change because it was hard to avoid with our lifestyle. I started to drink a lot more as well as eat way too much. Once again, to my surprise, the weight began to creep back on. On many occasions, Gary would whip up one of his amazing dinners, then we would enjoy some drinks together. We followed that up by smoking a joint, and only a few hours later, think it was a good idea to order a pizza. Now I'm not talking just your average pizza, I'm talking the real thick and heavy kind that leaves you feeling stuffed afterward. We felt as though we were living the good life, even though our credit cards were telling us otherwise. Not only was the weight pilling on, but so was our debt. Over time the pressure of living paycheque to paycheque started to take its toll. I would take the balance from one card and shift it to the other, trying to manage things as best as I could. I had kept up with our minimum payments, so our credit was also getting better, which allowed us to get more cards. We should have turned them down, but we figured we could manage.

One afternoon we decided maybe it would be a good idea to buy a condo instead of continuing to pay rent. We went into the bank and applied for a line of credit. We were instantly approved, so we were able to pay down some of our credit cards and were left with enough to put a down payment on a condo. Even though this put us further into debt, we looked at it like we had a bit of freedom again. In usual fashion, we would buy things we couldn't afford, making sure as long as we ended up with enough left to stock up on drinks for the week and have enough food in our fridge. To those on the outside, it probably seemed as though we did well for a living. Even though we shared one vehicle, we were always trading it in after a year and buying a new one. We purchased beautiful furniture and still showed up at events with food and drinks to share. Not realizing it back then, I think I just wanted to give people the impression we really had our shit together. This made things harder to manage emotionally because the reality of our situation was that even though we had all this stuff, our money was getting hard to manage, and we weren't able to afford this life. I started to experience depression again, which left me feeling hopeless and unsure of what to do. I would spend weekends attempting to blur out these feelings by getting drunk, but it only made things worse. Many nights after we decided to stay home we would have too much to drink and end up at the pub next door spending money we didn't have. So we would just continue to try and buy what we thought was happiness, which in reality led me down a dark path.

The first time we went out to go look at condos with our friend, who was our realtor, we found one we loved. It was on the first floor and had a deck that looked out to a grassy area with trees lining the border of the property. It was in a decent area of town and was within our budget. We had enough saved in our work investments along with a few thousand left on our line of credit that we were able to make an offer. We also justified the purchase because it would lower our monthly payments slightly, so we assumed we could use the extra couple hundred dollars to start paying off our credit cards. Of course, that did not happen because what do two alcoholics do with an extra couple hundred bucks? They go and buy more alcohol!!! Our offer was accepted, and we moved in a short time later. Things were really looking up, I thought, but I would soon realize this was just the beginning of things getting worse.

We decided it would be an excellent time to have a housewarming party to show off our new digs. In usual fashion, Gary outdid himself with appetizers and beverages for everyone that attended the party. People loved coming over to our place for that very reason because it was always a good time. One of our friends had bought us a big bottle of grey goose vodka to congratulate us on our new purchase. Even though we had planned on saving this for our own consumption, partway through the evening, I looked over at Gary, and he held the bottle up, asking who wanted shots. I was pretty wasted at the time, so it sounded like a great idea. Shortly after these shots from what I was told, I decided it would be a good idea to start performing lap dancing for some of our single guests. This wasn't abnormal for me because I was always the life of the party. Gary wasn't a big fan and looking back, I can't say I blame him even though I believed what I was doing was totally harmless. I loved any attention from men, and it didn't matter what form it came in, even if I was making the ass out of myself. I wasn't all that happy in my marriage, so any extra attention I got was ok by me. Trust me when I say there are more times than I would like to admit that I crossed the line. We weren't having sex very often anymore, and so I had decided to try and prove to myself that I was still attractive and that I still had it, even if that hurt Gary. The evening of the party ended with me near blackout, getting sick in our en-suite bathroom. Bev walked in and helped me get over to my bed. She looked at me and asked, "Why do you keep doing this to yourself?" I responded, "I don't know, but I promise this is the last time." By now, I had tears streaming down my face because when these kinds of questions came from Bev whom I respected more than anyone, I started to question what I was doing and where my life was heading. I had all the good intentions in the world to stop, and I had promised people I would, but the power of alcohol always canceled out those plans. No matter how many times I made that promise to people, I wasn't ready yet, and it was pretty evident by this time I wasn't going to be able to quit for someone else. When I told Bev that night that I was done, I meant every word of it. But a beer the next day would change all that as it usually did.

After we moved in, things went well for a short time. We had put a lot of effort into decorating the place just as we liked it and felt proud of our accomplishment. I, however, was starting to really feel the effects of my depression even more. I had gone through periods before where I felt as though something was wrong with me, but I chalked it up to my drinking and the debt we were in. This time around, it was becoming difficult to even enjoy a fun night out with friends. I would go into work, and what usually gave me a break from my personal life now started to blend together. Not only could I not keep it together at home, but the feelings of usefulness and despair began to flood into my work life. I laid in bed more evenings than I'd like to admit contemplating ending my life. I would think of ways to do it that would be quick and easy. I certainly didn't want to attempt it and fail either because then I would have to face everyone and explain why I never asked for help in the first place. My pride was too big, which maybe was a good thing because it gave me the pause I needed to reach out to someone eventually. I had faced depression before due to circumstances in my life, but this felt different. I could no longer explain why I felt so low other than life stuff, which so many other people also lived through. Even when things were right, I couldn't pick myself up. I remember one afternoon asking Bev if we could go out for a coffee and chat. I told her that nothing felt right, and it didn't matter what I did, but I just couldn't be happy. I was struggling with my marriage as well as my work life, and because of the debt we were in, I wasn't sure how much longer we could continue to pay our bills. She knew this had been going on longer than it should have so suggested I go and talk to a doctor about it, so I did. I would learn in the future that there is more depression in my family. My dad has dealt with it before, and today we can openly discuss it, which feels great.

As I sat at the doctor's office, filling out some forms that would rate me on a scale of being mildly depressed to severely depressed, I wasn't surprised that I came up high. When I went in to speak to my doctor, he took a look over the form and started to talk about options. I have massive respect for my doctor, who, by the way, is still my family doctor today. His first response was not writing me out a prescription, but instead, he talked about getting therapy.

After giving me a list of resources, asking me to join a program for people who suffer from anxiety and depression, as well as get a counselor, he prescribed with me some anti-depressant medication. He made it clear that the medication was only for a short period to help me increase my serotonin levels, but stressed that the most crucial part was that I did the work. He asked me to limit my drinking and explained to me that alcohol actually served as a depressant and would affect the medication I was on. I didn't see how that was possible because other than the hangover, alcohol made me feel normal. The reality was that by this time in my life, I wasn't even sure what normal was anymore. I went home that afternoon and was determined to create a better life for myself. I got a counselor right away and started working on the program that my doctor had recommended. After about a week on the medication, I began to notice how much happier I was feeling. I enjoyed the effects of the pills and was a little disappointed they would only be temporary. I didn't feel the need to continue counseling or the program I was working on after a few weeks because I thought that all I needed were those happy pills and life would be exceptional. People also started to notice a difference in my mood, so I felt as though I was back on track.

Gary and I began to get along again, and so one evening, we decided to have some friends over. As the night carried on, one of our friends brought up that we should all go to Las Vegas one weekend. It sounded like a fantastic idea. Actually, most of my grandest plans were always creating during a good drunk! An issue with Gary and I was that, after we had a few drinks, our responsible decision-making skills were utterly non-existent. I had just managed to start paying back some of the money we owed on our maxed-out credit cards, but luckily for us that evening, we had just enough to book a trip with our friends, so of course, we did. Yes, that's right, the little money we had left to buy food and household items we spent on a trip to Las Vegas with our friends. It seemed like a great idea at the time, and we figured we had a couple months to save up for the trip, so it felt worth it. For the record, the trip was a blast even though there are nights I don't remember. The first day we got there, I made it until about midafternoon before entering a blackout. Somehow I managed to get out of the pool and back to my room but ended up lying naked on the bathroom floor where a friend of mine found me. I remember her waking me up, saying, "Get up, bitch, we're going out!" All in all, I figured it was money well spent!

I'm not entirely sure why back then I assumed money and material things would make me feel happy, but we indeed came across to others like we were living this wonderful life. This was all an act because the truth was that we were two people who were really unhappy and only had one way to cope with the stress. I drank my feelings away and then had to deal with the guilt and remorse the next day, so I would repeat this cycle again and again. Back then, I wanted to have it all, or at least that's what I thought I should have had at that age. Marriage, cars, a new condo, a puppy, and vacations did not provide the fulfilling life I thought it would. In fact, the more stuff I added to my life, the more empty I started to feel. Nothing would fix the void inside of me. I had been filled with resentment towards Gary. I just couldn't own the fact that this was my fault just as much as it was his. Since this time, I have learned that I'm actually so much happier with less. I don't need all that stuff in my life to feel whole. In fact, I learned to fill this void in a more healthy way, which I'll get into a bit later.

Lessons Learned:

* Getting drunk right after you have surgery is not a very good idea.
* I learned that codependency ran deep in all my relationships. As I result later in life, I would learn to create more healthy boundaries.
* I learned that just because I had credit didn't mean I should use it.
* I thought that having more material things would bring

me happiness. It really didn't. Less was actually more.

Final Thoughts:

Have you ever felt as though money and material items would fix it all? If you have, I'd love to hear your story about how you overcame this belief.

Email me at info@theroadtohealth.me

Suggested Solution:

When I started to live with less, I felt as though I had more of what I needed in life. A few times a year, I go through my belongings and donate what I no longer need. It's a very cleansing process!

**Suggested Solution:**

When I started to live with less, I felt as though I had more of what I needed in life. A few times a year, I go through my belongings and donate what I no longer need. It's a very cleansing process!

## THE DIGGING STOPS

In early 2011, Gary and I were in a lot of debt. We had owned our condo for about five years and continued to add credit card debt on top of what we already owed. Any time we qualified for more credit, we would use the new to pay off the old. We even decided that buying another vehicle we couldn't afford was a great idea, and this happened following an afternoon at the pub. As I said, grand plans came as a result of my drinking. The debt started to become another considerable strain on our relationship. I had only been off my antidepressants for a short time, and I could feel the anxiety and depression start to creep back in due to the stress. There were weekends that I would look at our statements and realize we only had enough money after all the bills were paid to buy a large bottle of vodka, a little bit of food, and some gas to get to work. It was probably a good thing we only had one vehicle at the time because there is no way we could have afforded two. Until this point, we usually had a little extra money available on our credit cards to spend, so although I knew we were in debt, it still felt as though we had choices. That is the danger of accepting a new card when all your others are at their limit. Now it was starting to feel as though we did not have a way out. I felt as though the walls were closing up around me, and I could hardly breathe. Gary was offered a lot of overtime at work, yet for some reason, he didn't believe in working the extra hours. I, on the other hand, was salary paid so it didn't matter how much I worked I wasn't bringing home any extra money to help support our unhealthy spending habits. One afternoon at work, I was so stressed out about our debt that I texted Gary to meet me outside in front of the shop. My boss knew my situation because it was clear I was struggling in my home life. He had let me know that they could use Gary to work an extra shift that weekend but that he had turned down the offer again. When Gary met me outside, I asked him why he continued to turn down the overtime he was offered. I told him he was selfish because we needed the money, and there was nothing I could do other than get a second job to contribute more myself. He looked at me and said, "I don't want to work anymore than I have to, so no, I'm not doing it." I looked at him as tears started to roll down my face and the anger built inside of me. "Why would you not help get us out of the debt we've managed to get ourselves in?" He replied by saying, "I'm not sure. Figure it out!" The pain I felt inside me only increased with this response. I was so hurt and angry and blurted something out that at that very moment, I meant with my entire being. "If you don't start working overtime to help get us out of this debt, I am going to kill myself, make it look like an accident so you can use our insurance money to get your shit together without me." We both stood there in silence as I continued to sob. The look on his face was one of shock. I needed him to know how serious this was getting. We were in a hole that I didn't feel we could dig ourselves out of anymore. After a moment of silence, he said, "I'll think about it." He turned around and walked back inside.

Gary would eventually end up working the extra hours, but now it felt as though he was carrying a lot of resentment towards me. I didn't care because I felt as though he was super selfish anyways. He never attempted to get counseling to improve our marriage or with his own problems. We had started to grow apart over the last couple of years. Both of us gained a lot of weight, although Gary was making an effort to lose some of it. It did help that we couldn't afford to buy much food. I, on the other hand, continued to gain weight, which just added to my depression and insecurities. Anytime we had a little extra cash, and Gary wasn't around, I would run across the street and buy a burger and fries because it gave me that instant gratification I was seeking. It wasn't only alcohol that I used to numb my feelings. I had gained 75 pounds and couldn't even look at myself in the mirror without feeling disgusted. How could I have let myself go like this!? I thought. It was no wonder why Gary didn't want to have sex with me anymore. I believe we had now gone for about six months without any. So needless to say, I didn't feel attractive anymore. One afternoon I confronted him about this and asked him if my weight gain played a role in our sex life to which he answered, "Yes, it does." The worst part was that it wasn't as though I was the only one who had let myself go over the last few years. I was crushed by his honesty and felt as though I had hit a new bottom. I was already the type of person who felt less than, but now those feelings had just been further validated by the man who loved me the most.

I started down a path of shame and guilt, so I covered up those feelings the only way I knew how. I would start to drink even more when we went out with friends, and my flirting began to grow as I sought out the attention of other men to prove I was still attractive. It wasn't like I did this behind Gary's back either. I remember I took on a part-time job as a financial advisor that year to attempt to help out with the bills. Ok, let me just say, yes, you heard that right. I was now in the worst debt of my life and helping others manage theirs. I wasn't all that bad at it either, but it was a little F'd up! Regardless I was attempting to get us out of debt. I enjoyed it most because there was also a social aspect of being an advisor. The company I worked for hosted a lot of events. I met a lot of amazing people through these events and enjoyed the times we spent together. It became like a second family for me. We went on many trips to attend conferences. Some of those places included Los Angeles, Las Vegas, and we even filled up a minivan one weekend and drove 10 hours to Banff, Alberta. This time of my life certainly helped to take the focus off my marriage due to how little I was home.

If there was one thing I had learned from this industry, it was that they knew how to party, and they did it well. Many events offered free booze, which I loved. There were also times like in Las Vegas, where the financial institutions would rent out night clubs for an evening to host an afterparty. It was no wonder why I loved this world so much. I fit right in! For the first time in a long time, I felt as though I might make something of myself! I believed that this was my big break, and I would end up wealthy after all of this. Can you see how those grand plans come back into the picture? I would always dream big, but there was never much action to go along with that dream. Oh, how I loved the magic of alcohol. Hey, at least it took away the doom and gloom feeling for a short time, right?

One of the banks we did business with decided to host a party around the holidays. Gary and I attended together, which didn't happen very often, and trust me when I say it was usually much safer that way. I had a way of acting out that, for the most part, I thought was harmless, but I can tell you if I saw Gary pulling some of the stunts I did, I would have lost my shit! At this particular party, I got very drunk. Gary was being a little anti-social and wanted to go home, but I wanted to take full advantage of the open bar. Towards the end of the evening, I decided it was a good idea to start dancing and then to add to this, provide some lap dances to some of the guys. Now, this was not abnormal behavior during a party when Gary was not with me, but I probably should have considered that before I started to act out in front of him. We left very abruptly after that because Gary was less than impressed by my behavior, but I was too drunk to care. He asked me how I could disrespect him like this to which I answered, "Well, you don't want me anyway, so what does it matter!" We had a friend with us that evening, and although I don't remember most of the ride home, I do remember asking Gary to pull over on the highway so I could get sick. The world started to spin, and I didn't think I could wait another few minutes until we got home. Gary wouldn't stop because he was so angry, and so I asked him again. No response, so I slowly started to roll the window down and stuck my head out of the car. I won't get into the gory details to spare you any meals you may have eaten recently, but it was terrible. I had a big mess to clean up the following morning, and Gary would not let me live that evening down. I decided to wash up by getting into the bath fully clothed that night, and because of his anger, Gary left me there. I woke up that next morning with cold water up to my chin. As bad as this sounds, I certainly do not blame Gary for leaving me in these situations. I was very disrespectful towards him towards the end of our marriage, and I pushed his patience right over the edge on many occasions. He was always the one left to pick up the mess.

I started to feel burnt out working two jobs, and so I finally decided to stop doing the financial advising. I was sad to leave what felt like family, but due to the amount of drinking we all did together, it also started to create a lot of unnecessary drama in my life that I didn't need. I was depressed, unhappily married, overweight, and overworked. I continued to disappoint Gary with my flirtatious behavior, which only made things worse, so I knew something had to give. I suggested going to counseling, which I had done many times in the past, but Gary rejected the idea. I wasn't exactly sure how we were going to save our marriage anymore, but as always, I had a solution to solve my problems.

One afternoon I decided I was tired of fighting, so I went to visit a friend. We had been friends since elementary school, and although we didn't see each other much anymore, it still always felt as though we could pick up where we left off. We caught up over a bottle of wine as I told her what was going on with my relationship. One bottle led to another, and suddenly all was right in the world again. I had promised Gary I would be home by dinner, but I was having too much fun catching up to keep my promise. Shocker, I know! After our second bottle of wine, my friend asked me a question that shocked me a little at that moment. "Hey, did you want to grab a little coke?" I was only surprised by this question because ten years earlier, she had begged me to stop using. I hadn't consumed any hard drugs for eight years now because I knew where it led me. The question alone gave me feelings of excitement, and it didn't help that we were already two bottles in because, as I've mentioned, my decision-making skills are not at their best when I'm drinking. Even though I knew this was a bad idea, I couldn't pass up the opportunity. We went out and bought some and did a few lines at her place before heading out for dinner. The second I ingested that amazing white powder; I felt as though I came alive again. All my problems with Gary melted away. In fact, who was Gary!? I hadn't even bothered to call him and let him know I wasn't coming home that evening. When cocaine was involved, nothing else seemed to matter. I ended up crashing at my friend's place that night, and when I got home, I received an earful. I knew I was taking a risk and jeopardizing my marriage by using again, but things were so bad already that I didn't feel they could get any worse. There was no effort to make things better, and so I thought I might as well enjoy myself.

The only time we showed signs of still being happily married somewhat was when we started an evening out with a few drinks. Gary was a very functioning alcoholic, so he would always hit a point where he wanted to go home and go to bed to pass out. I, however, was not and had no off switch. Typically I would buy myself a 12 or 18 pack of beer for the evening and also have some of Gary's vodka as a backup. You would think this would tie me over for an entire evening, but it did not. Most nights right before I knew the liquor store was about to close, I would head out and make another beer run. I certainly didn't need anymore, nor should I even have been driving to get there, but I wanted to be sure I was never left short. It was usually right after that I would blackout. I would wake up the following day with Gary mad at me all over again because of something stupid I had said or done, and this is how the cycle continued. My blackouts started to get worse because of how depressed I was, and so I decided it was time to add some cocaine back into the mix. I had done it a few short weeks prior and enjoyed it, so I figured it couldn't hurt. It also helped me not to blackout as much, so really, it was a win-win. I knew it was a slippery slope, but once I opened the door, it was hard to turn back. I started using again and sneaking it behind Gary's back. I'm not sure if he ever knew I was using again, but to be honest, I wasn't all that concerned about the consequences anymore. The problem with cocaine was that it only amplified my depression and made things so much worse.

My stress started to escalate, and it showed in my work and personal life. I hated myself for the person I had become. I spent a lot of time contemplating life, my role in this world, and how much better this world would be without me in it. I think deep down inside; I knew a lot of the issues in our marriage were my fault. I got married in the first place because I thought it would make me whole. I believed that having a ring on my finger would make things all better when, in fact, all it did was keep us together longer so that we could continue to make each other even more miserable. I felt as though I was now out of options. I was a depressed, overweight alcoholic with the inability to handle life. Drinking had always been my solution to managing what life threw at me, and now it wasn't working anymore. Night after night, because of my actions, I felt substantial feelings of guilt and remorse. I wasn't doing my part to make anything any better, but I wasn't sure how to either. For the first time, I felt genuinely hopeless, and I didn't want to be part of this life anymore.

Little did I realize at the time, but this would be the bottom I would need to hit to start making positive changes. I had reached many so-called bottoms throughout my life, but this is the one that made me stop digging. The hole I had dug for myself was too deep, and I felt as though I couldn't get out of it. I didn't see the light at the end of the tunnel anymore. I needed a way out, and so one night, I said a little prayer even though back then I didn't believe anymore. I said, "God, I need help, and I'm not sure what to do anymore." I left it at that and hoped that whatever the outcome, it would free me from the pain I felt.

**Lessons Learned:**

* My bottom came when I decided to stop digging. I realized no measure determines if you've hit bottom. That was for me to decide and me alone.
* Marriage did not make me whole, nor did living a life I thought was expected from society.
* I did not have to be like everyone else, I needed to figure out who I was and what I truly wanted in life and then live it.

**Final Thoughts:**

Have you ever felt so lost and hopeless that you assumed there was no way out? I understand this feeling very well, so if you want to share your story about this, let me know.

You can email me at info@theroadtohealth.me

**Suggested Solution:**

Thoughts of suicide are severe and not to be ignored. Reach out for help. I made a mistake in my early year not to ask for the help I needed. If you are struggling with these thoughts, please do not wait.

## THERE IS A PLAN

As I sat on the floor, pills in hand, tears in my eyes, I said to my dog, "Life would just be easier if I weren't in it." As selfish as that might sound, I was tired of hurting those around me. I hated repeating the words; I'm done, I promise I won't drink like that anymore. Rudy, my pug, looked up at me at that moment and tilted his head ever so slightly. With that look, I felt as though Rudy could see right into my soul and was begging me to give life one more chance. That was my bottom moment because it was the day I stopped digging.

Like most people do on January 1st, I decided it was time to make a New Year's resolution. I had made many before this that had never materialized after the first month, but this time it felt different. I felt inspired to change, so I did what many people do those early few days of January, and I got myself a gym membership. I was determined to stay consistent this time and so made a plan to go at least three days a week. I started strong, but then after about a month, I felt as though I wasn't making progress and had no idea what I was doing. I had worked out before but thought to myself, If I want to make any real progress, I would need to ask for help. The excitement was wearing off quickly, and I didn't feel I could hold up my momentum much longer. On my way out of the gym, I noticed an ad for personal training. I wrote her email address down and decided it was time to reach out and ask someone for help. Doing things alone wasn't serving me very well, so this seemed like a sensible solution.

I turned on my computer and waited for it to load up. I thought to myself; I can't believe I'm asking for help! Shouldn't an adult be able to do this stuff alone by now?? Well, my friends, I have done a lot of things on my own and look where it got me. I wrote a message, knowing that I had to suck up my pride for things to change. As I explained who I was, why I needed the help, and asked how much it would cost me, I experienced a sense of relief. It felt good to ask for assistance, and it felt as though a weight had been lifted off my shoulders. I finished up my message and breathed a sigh of relief. It was time to feel good about myself again. Shortly after I sent the request, I received a reply. To my surprise, the trainer I had reached out to asked what high school I went to. I posted a response, and it turned out that we went to the same school for a brief period and took gymnastics together. I pulled out my yearbook, and instantly I remembered who she was. What a small world! I thought. We set up a date to meet and go over what it took to get started the following week. Little did I know at the time that this meeting would change the course of my life. Remember back in my story when I was in high school, and I mentioned meeting a couple of people that would have an impact on my life in the future? Well, apart from Bev, who was still my best friend, Becky was also one of those people.

I went to the gym and was excited to get started. Becky and I caught up for a short time and laughed about our mutual gymnastics experience back in high school. From what we could remember, neither one of us excelled in gymnastics, so we had a good laugh about it all. It was nice to be working with someone I felt comfortable around. As Becky went through the list of questions to figure out our starting point, she asked, "So what is the number one goal you'd like to achieve?" I sat and thought about it for a minute and then said, "Well, I have always wanted to be comfortable in my own skin, so I would have to say I'd love to be able to fit into a bikini." I had a dream of going to Las Vegas and being poolside while feeling comfortable. I thought about how amazing it would feel laying poolside, drink in my hand, the music blaring, and weighing about 80 pounds lighter. I was determined to make this happen.

As I started on this new journey, I was excited about the new life I was going to create for myself. At that time in my life, I truly believed that if I could look better on the outside, then it would fix the pain and insecurity I was experiencing on the inside. I had to start making some essential adjustments to my lifestyle because I had to make sure I went all-in on this transformation as I did with many other things. First off, I had to get rid of all the junk food in the house because my new way of eating was fresh whole foods. I needed to make sure there were no temptations anywhere. The second thing is it was recommended I only drink black coffee, tea, and water. This was going to be a challenge for me because although I had tried coffee before a couple of times, I didn't enjoy it even with lot's a cream and sugar in it. I looked at my options and decided to force myself to drink coffee. At least the caffeine buzz would provide me some sort of instant gratification. Of course, I drank water along with it, but I needed some added energy to get me through my day. Here is where it got tricky; how was I going to fit alcohol in?? You see, at the time, I made the decision that I was going to be healthy and only drink on the weekends; I still hadn't realized that I even had a problem with alcohol or that I could be even considered an alcoholic. I had existed like this for so long now, that it seemed normal. I decided I was going to buy a case of beer every Friday, and I would only allow myself to drink three of those beers per evening and only on the weekends. It felt like a good plan moving and one I thought I could stick too.

The first month of my new lifestyle went great! I shared my plan with all my friends, and I received the "Good for you!" response. For some reason, I had the feeling some of them didn't believe this was going to happen. I can't say I blame them either because I had made a lot of empty promises. Instead of spending a whole evening with friends, my husband and I only spent a small portion of the afternoon and then went home for dinner. This plan made drinking only three beers per day a lot easier to start. Every Sunday afternoon, I would do my food prep and make sure I had all my meals laid out and easy to grab. My staples became chicken, broccoli, and rice, sometimes adding green beans into the mix. I would add in a couple of servings of fruits, and for the most part, early on, I enjoyed it. I was finally starting to see some results as well, so that made me feel even better about my meal choices. I trained with Becky one day a week and made sure I was a good student and went to the gym as often as I could apart from our training. On Saturdays I was able to enjoy a cheat meal, which I obsessed about most of the week because I wanted it to be epic every time. If I was only allowed to have one, I had to make the most of it. I think back today and believe that the reason I also did so well is that I was trying to impress others. I wanted that gold star and to be recognized for my achievements. I needed the recognition from others to feel good about myself.

As time went on, I started missing my weekend routines with friends. It was spring now, and although I was down about thirty pounds and my results were driving me to continue, I still felt as though with summer right around the corner, it was only going to get more difficult. The following weekend we decided to stay at our friend's place through dinner, which we hadn't done a lot since I started my weight loss journey. I decided to have a couple of extra beers before we left to tie me over for a short time, but the extras just made the desire to have more even worse. I asked my husband if we could go home and although he wasn't super happy with my request at the time, he obliged and off we went. The slight buzz I had was making it difficult to cut myself off; I so badly wanted another drink. I had been doing so well so far and didn't want to screw things up as I usually did. When I start to see results after a time, I can quickly develop complacency. I tend to relax on my program and cut myself more slack, which results in me having to start over again. I went into the bathroom after we got home and found a bottle of NyQuil. Perfect, I thought. I drank almost half the bottle and joined my husband on the couch until I started to fall asleep. I had found a solution to cut myself off early when the cravings got too much. I was a genius!

By April 2012, Becky and I had become friends outside of our training. I was very proud of the lifestyle I had adopted up until that point because I knew as soon as I hit my goal, I would be a brand new person full of confidence. Although I would love to say I thought of this as a permanent lifestyle change when I started, that would be a lie. I looked at this as a temporary sacrifice that I was determined to make. As our friendship grew, I quickly discovered that Becky didn't drink. I didn't know anyone who didn't enjoy alcohol even if it was only once in a while. We had gone out for coffee many times, but on the occasion we went out for dinner, I never saw her order a drink. I attempted to be respectful of our friendship and followed suit by ordering a diet coke; after all, I could drink when I got home. I think I may have questioned her once about it and all she said was that she didn't drink anymore. I left it at that because I didn't feel as if it was any of my business. I just remembered trying to play the role of someone who didn't drink often, but I would come to find out that Becky saw right through that.

In June, I was in full swing with my new healthy lifestyle and had lost about forty pounds. I felt great and started to feel like I was in control of this life I had created for myself. The weekends were a struggle, but I was obsessed at this point, I saw the finish line, and I wasn't about to give up now. At this point, my marriage was starting to become a little strained. I only focused on losing weight, and although my husband wasn't against the idea, I wasn't the same person he had met nine years earlier. Our communication started to lack, and unless he had had a few drinks in him, we didn't have a lot to say to each other. It created a lot of distance between us, but it wasn't something that worried me at the time because I had only one thing on my mind, and that was to hit my goal weight. I wasn't going to let anything get in my way, including my marriage.

During the process, I felt as though I was becoming a better person. I was so obsessed with losing weight that my old life was starting to slip away slowly. I no longer went out every weekend with friends, it had been months since I'd experience a blackout, and to be honest, it felt good. I also think at this point, I had now justified that I did not have a problem with drinking because if I did have an issue, there was no way I would be able to go this long with only having nine drinks every weekend. I was so proud of this accomplishment that I wasn't afraid to share it with anyone I knew. It was as though I was trying to convince them that I didn't have a drinking problem. Here is the thing I learned years later, people who do not suffer from alcoholism do not spend time sharing with others how little they were able to drink over the weekend. Most people don't care, but I did! After all, it was a significant accomplishment. I would have shouted from the rooftops if I could have.

I felt so good at that point that I wanted to do something out of my comfort zone. I figured I was a whole new person, so I was going to do something big. Becky and I had been talking about going sky diving or bungee jumping, so I called her up and said, "Let's book it! Let's go bungee jumping!" She agreed, and on June 9th, 2012, off we went. It was a beautiful drive up to Whistler, BC, and it allowed Becky and I some time to chat about life. On the ride, I remember getting into a conversation about our lifestyles. I shared some of the stupid things I had done in my life, and of course, most of it involved drugs and alcohol. I also used these substances to justify a lot of my actions. This topic, of course, led me to ask again why she didn't drink. She told me that she had gotten sober three years prior, and it was the best choice she had ever made. Becky shared some of her experiences with me and also how she managed to get sober. I remember thinking, good for her, I'm glad she was able to turn her life around, but that's not something I need to do because I've already done so on my own. She told me that if I was ever interested in looking into sobriety to let her know and we left it at that. Of course, I didn't think I had a problem; after all, I was only drinking nine bottles of beer per weekend! That is nowhere near what an alcoholic would drink and the NyQuil, well, no one had to know about that.

We made it to our destination, and I was scared out of my mind. Walking up to the point where you jumped off a bridge into a canyon didn't seem as appealing from when we booked it. I felt as though I was going to get sick, but I came here for a reason, and I was going to jump even if it killed me on the way down. The experience was one I would never forget. I couldn't believe that I had conquered one of my fears because I was terrified of heights. I felt as though things were going to change from this day forward, and boy did they ever, but not before one last weekend away with my husband.

The following weekend my husband and I had planned to take a trip out of town. We booked a home overlooking the ocean and planned a weekend of mountain biking, hiking, and relaxing. It was the first time I had gone away since I started training. I was used to spending my weekends at the gym or getting out early on Saturday morning to participate in a boot camp. On the way out of town, we made a stop at the liquor store. I figured since we had a view of the ocean, it would be appropriate to bring some wine with us, so I grabbed a bottle for myself. I had displayed such willpower recently that I was sure one bottle of wine would last me the entire weekend. Of course, my husband decided to come prepared as we always had when we went away and grabbed some rum, vodka, beer, and a box of red wine just in case. We were excited to go and spend some time together because things hadn't been the same since I started my lifestyle change back in February of that year. I was so focused on getting in shape that our relationship fell to the wayside.

We arrived at our destination around noon and decided it would be good to start our day off with a hike. The weather was beautiful, and at the top of this hike, there was a gorgeous view of the ocean. I also wanted to get a bit of a workout in, and this was the perfect way to do it. I started to think how nice it would be to have a glass of wine and sit looking at the ocean, so we made our way back. The home we had rented had a hot tub, which came in handy because we were both a little sore from the hike. I opened up the bottle of white wine and poured a glass. I slipped on my bathing suit and slid into the hot tub. That first sip of wine relaxed me instantly. Since February, I had only really only drunk beer because wine gave me a buzz quicker, and I knew it would be harder to control. I felt a sense of comfort and ease come over me with every sip after, and before I knew it, the bottle was empty. I felt great, and we were having such a good time. Of course, we never left anywhere short-handed when it came to alcohol, so I knew we had plenty to tie us over. I started in on the box of red wine. By about 5 pm, we decided it would probably be a good idea to go and grab something to eat, so we drove down to the local pub and feasted on some oysters and other delicious seafood. We had a great time and became friends with some of the locals by the end of the night. I remember getting the bar tab and thinking Holy shit! How did our bill amount to $200! Oh well, it was what it was, and so we went back to our little retreat on the ocean. We enjoyed some more drinks in the hot tub from what I can remember until the night became a little foggy. After that, I don't recall a thing.

I woke up the following morning with a pounding headache. The minute I lifted my head off the pillow, I had this overwhelming wave of nausea come over me. I got up as quickly as I could and stumbled to the washroom. I had a hard time walking straight because I was still drunk, but I made it just in time. I couldn't believe how awful I felt. I managed to make my way back to bed and wanted to die. I was so confident in my ability to stick with my one bottle of wine that weekend. Now we were almost out of all the alcohol we had brought for both nights. Gary didn't take into consideration that I would be drinking more than I said I would. I knew the only thing to do was to have a drink, and this would calm my nerves and at least get me through the day. By around 3 pm I felt good as new, we went down to the liquor store to re-stock for the evening, and this time we made a promise we would stay at the house and just relax and play some cards. Needless to stay, I can't remember much of that evening; it was pretty apparent that I had a problem.

The following morning I woke up in the same shape I had the morning before. My head was pounding, and I had a hard time seeing straight. My husband offered me a glass of wine to clear up my hangover, but this time I said no. Instead, I asked him if he could hand me my phone. I sat there, not understanding how things got so out of control. I was so sure that I would be able to limit the number of drinks I had because I had been so strong for months now. Tears started to flow from my face because, for the first time in months, I felt completely out of control again. It all happened so quickly, and I never saw it coming. I had so much pride in myself that asking for help was the last thing I wanted to do. I picked up my phone and sent a text to the only person I knew at the time could help me. I started typing the words, "I need help, can I still take you up on your offer?", to which she responded, "Yes, of course." June 17th, 2012, was the day I began my journey into sobriety.

I believe that some people are put into our path for a reason, and it's up to us to recognize what those reasons are and accept the opportunities as they present themselves. I reached out for help at the right time that year to the right person, and although weight loss had become a struggle for me, that wasn't the central issue in my life. I battled addiction of all kinds, especially alcoholism, and on that day back in February, I reached out to someone who would guide me down a very different path from the one I had been on for so long.

**Lessons Learned:**

* I believe that people come into our lives for a reason. When I remain open-minded as to what those reasons are, things start to change.
* It's ok to not be ok! We just have to find the strength to ask for help.
* Opportunities present themselves to us when we least expect them, and I personally have missed many. I learned to always keep myself open to the possibilities of something new.
* When I tried to control things so that they would go my way, they often went the complete opposite.

**Final Thoughts:**

Have you ever had someone come into your life at the right time, which triggered a series of events in which your life changed?

I'd love to hear your story! Info@theroadtohealth.me

**Suggested Solution:**

Learning to stay open-minded has been an essential addition to my life. Take the time to listen more than you speak. You may hear something that will have a significant impact on your life.

Recommended Exercise: 24 hours of silence. No electronics. Yup, you heard me! I could only do things like reading, journaling, meditation, prayer. It wasn't easy, but it was worth it.

* See Tips & Resources
* Bonus Offer for Readers!
* Wake Up on Fire Workshop (FREE) www.theroadforward.ca

## SOBRIETY

My journey through early sobriety wasn't an easy one. I was a stubborn person, lacked faith, and in all honesty, I wasn't at all sure how I was going to live a sober life. I had known nothing else since the age of 14, so mostly I had to learn how to be a productive member of society. There was one thing I did learn very quickly after I decided to give this new way of life a try. Gary and I had nothing to talk about when both of us were sober. As I started to work on myself and learn what it meant to take responsibility for my life, he grew full of resentment. He would often remind me that he wanted nothing to do with my new way of life. It was incredibly frustrating living with someone who drank every day and had no concern over how that might make me feel. I knew I couldn't force him into living sober with me, but the amount of push back I got surprised me. He had gotten so mad every time I got drunk that I honestly thought he would look at this as a blessing. Boy, was I wrong!

One afternoon as we drove home from work together, I told him how much it hurt me that he wasn't willing to support me in any way. Gary replied by saying to me that he did encourage me but didn't want me to assume he would also have to make these changes. He was happy with who he was and didn't want to give me false hope that one day he would change as well. Even though I knew I couldn't force Gary to make the same changes I was, I guess I had hoped he would. I pointed out that he drank every night, and because it was early on in my sobriety, this made me want to spend even more time away from home. Our relationship was already strained enough, and I assumed that just maybe if I could get my shit together, things would improve. I told him I would stop bugging him about the subject if he would agree to give me one evening without alcohol. I begged him for one night so that maybe we could start to make our marriage work again. Reluctantly he agreed, and so that Friday, we made plans to go out for dinner. For the first time in a long time, I had a small glimmer of hope that just maybe we could save our marriage before it completely fell apart.

I don't exactly remember where we ended up going for dinner that night, but after work, we both got ready and jumped in the car. Gary was quiet, and I could tell he was very uncomfortable from not having his usual post-work drinks to wind down. I do know how it feels to have a routine for twenty plus years and then suddenly stop, and Gary certainly needed something to wind down after work because of how worked up he got. We didn't say much on the car ride over to the restaurant. I could tell that Gary was moody and resented me for asking him not to have a drink that night. I started to feel even more guilty, and it had me questioning if I had made the right decision. Shortly after we arrived, we were seated and ordered a couple of diet cokes. As hard as I tried to keep the conversation going, I very soon realized that we had nothing to talk about. Everything felt so forced, and nothing was happening naturally. I felt as though I was on a horrible first date, and I'm pretty sure the waiter felt the tension between us as well. We made quick work of dinner, settled the bill, and went home. As soon as we walked in the door, Gary turned around and said. "There, are you happy?" He then proceeded to go to the fridge to pour himself a vodka soda and sat down in front of the TV. At that moment, I knew our marriage was over. The reality was that I was responsible for my own life, and no matter how badly I wanted this to be for both of us, it was my journey. That night I knew my sobriety was something I had to continue to put work into. I was done with feeling depressed and hopeless.

I decided to take a trip down to San Jose, CA, to spend some time with a mutual friend of ours. I had met Kathy through Gary when we first started dating, and she and I had become very close over the last nine years. The trip gave me some time to think about my options and also to receive some feedback. Kathy knew Gary well, so when I told her about our situation, she wasn't all that surprised.

Gary was stubborn and very set in his ways. During my visit, I wrote out a list of pros and cons for staying in the relationship. I knew I had to have a good honest conversation with Gary about our future, and so I wrote down the questions I wanted to address. The problem was that when I got emotional or felt as though I was backed into a corner, I started to unravel. Gary was very reactive, so often, a straightforward conversation turned into a high-intensity argument. I needed to be ready for anything he responded with, so being prepared was a requirement.

Before I had the conversation with Gary, I had to make one more stop. Becky had been helping me get through my first couple of months of sobriety, and so I wanted to run what I had come up with by her first. I was very well known for making snap decisions without running them by someone first. The results of these decisions usually didn't come with the same outcome as I would anticipate. They would often turn out completely different than I had planned and so I started to wise up to the fact that just maybe I should run my ideas by someone first. After showing Becky my list as well as the questions, I was going to confront Gary with, she laughed and told me. "Do not bring up the pro's and con's list!" Even though I thought it was such a smart idea at the time I wrote it, it was pointed out to me that I shouldn't be bringing up what is right and wrong about Gary if I wanted to have a productive conversation. Yup, I could see now how that may not go over well, so I scrapped that list. There was one more thing to discuss before I went home to have this tough conversation. "Where am I going to live if this doesn't work out?" I asked Becky. I was so broke and knew I didn't have the money to move out on my own. Becky responded, "Why don't you come to stay with us? We have an extra bedroom, so you are welcome until you can get back on your feet again." I knew this was a safe place for me and the only option, so I accepted. It was then that I made the firm decision that I needed to leave and give myself the space to determine if my marriage was worth it.

That afternoon I walked in the front door of our condo and sat down on one of the bar stools that was located in the kitchen and overlooked the living room. Gary was in his usual spot in front of the TV, having a drink, and playing video games. He looked up and said, "Hi, babe! What's up? How was your day?" I was doing everything I could to hold back the tears because I was dreading the conversation that I was about to have. "Can you turn off the TV for a few minutes so we can talk?" He did as I asked, and I'm pretty sure he was well aware of what was about to happen. After all, it was no surprise that our marriage had been falling apart for some time now. I held onto the piece of paper shaking and started to read what I had written down out loud. As I worked through my notes, I felt as though I was having an out of body experience. Tears were streaming down my face as I faced the reality that after this conversation, my marriage might be over. I finished up and started to sob uncontrollably. I looked up at Gary and fully expected him to lash out with frustration over what I had just said. Instead, he sat there with sadness in his eyes and said. "I understand how you feel, and I will support the decision you want to make. Do what you have to do." I may have gone into shock for a brief moment because having Gary agree with me wasn't something that happened often. Usually, we would butt heads because of our differences in opinions, but this time he didn't fight back. I think both of us were so tired of fighting and knew that the break would do us well. Even though I had a pretty good idea that our marriage was over for good, I knew Gary still had the hope in him that given some space, I may change my mind. I told him that I needed a few days to pack my things and that by the end of the week, I would be gone. Surprisingly, we had an enjoyable last few days together. He didn't drink as much, and we had some great conversations. I started to second guess my decision, but with the help of some very supportive friends, I stuck to my choice and left when I said I would.

The day I left was an emotional one. Gary helped me pack, and we went and brought the last of my stuff out to the car.

I went back inside to grab that last box as well as say goodbye. As I walked to the door and turned around, I saw Gary and my dog, Rudy standing there looking at me with sadness in their eyes. This moment will forever be etched into my memory, and even as I write this, I can still feel the sadness and emotions that I felt back then. I truly loved Gary, and just maybe had we both not been alcoholics, things would have turned out differently between us. Then again, things always seem to turn out only like they are meant to, and I believe this was no different. There is no doubt in my mind that Gary loved me, but I knew from experience now that to change, you had to have the desire to do so. Gary was happy with who he was and the life we had built, but this was a lifestyle I just didn't want to live anymore. The drive over to Becky's place was a blur. I pulled into the driveway and almost dropped to my knees; I was so upset. I had nine years of memories come flooding back into my head all at once. The sadness I experienced was like no other because before this, I had always had a solution to deal with my pain. I was no longer able to take a drink to make this all go away, and so for the next few days, I cried and cried until I felt as though I couldn't possibly have any tears left in me. Although it was a very healing process, I didn't feel comfortable at all with these new emotions. I'm grateful I had finally chosen a way to learn how to experience and deal with them.

Over the next month, I started to put a lot of work into myself and my sobriety. I took a good look at my past and began to see how my addiction had taken over and affected others. It was important I could see just how unmanageable life became when I drank or used drugs so that I wouldn't repeat these behaviors in the future. I had friends who guided me as well as support networks that helped me understand what I was going through along the way. It was also suggested to me by Becky that I start to develop faith and gain an acceptance that just maybe there is something greater than myself out there. The problem for me was that I had built up a sort of prejudice around religion and didn't believe there was a God, so having to admit I may have been wrong didn't sit well. Although I didn't want to admit it, I was still trying to run my life my way, which, as we know, doesn't always work out for the best. Let's be honest, look at where that control got me! I was determined to do anything I could to change my life, and so I took the suggestion of my friend and gave this whole higher power thing a shot. I knew something had to change because I felt as though I was white-knuckling it at times and barely hanging on. I certainly didn't want to go back to the way things were.

As I was figuring out how to accept a higher power into my life, I decided it might be time to attend a few church services. I wasn't sure I wanted religion or God in my life back then, but I knew that I didn't want to go back to the life I was living previously. I prayed the evening before the service and asked to receive a sign that it was ok to let God guide me. So I got down on my knees and started to pray to something I didn't yet understand. I was struggling to stay sober at the time, and so I prayed that if there was indeed a God that I would receive a sign that it was ok to stop controlling my life. I went on to ask that the sign wasn't subtle either because I needed something reasonably big and obvious so that I wouldn't miss it. I continued praying to attempt not to be selfish and instead ask for guidance and help.

The next morning Becky and I went to the service together. I wasn't at the point where I wanted to go alone, so being there with a friend certainly helped. As we sat down, the church youth pastor stepped out on the stage. He was subbing into today, and he was also easy on the eyes. As he started to speak, the words that came out of his mouth still make me emotional today. I felt as though he was looking right at me and talking to me as though I was the only person in the room. His words reached my soul and moved me. The subject that day was letting go and letting God. I had a hard time fighting back the tears as emotions started to swell inside me. Everything I had prayed about the night before was being answered on that very stage. I felt a sense of comfort that morning that I had only felt previously from alcohol, except this time was different. There was no having to hide my emotions or mask my feelings; all of a sudden, I felt as though I could let go of this massive weight I had been carrying on my shoulders for years. I felt as though I was at peace, and I no longer had to worry about controlling everything. It felt as though at that moment, I had accepted that no matter what life throws at me, my needs would always be met. This was my first real experience of faith, and wow did it hit me like a ton of bricks. After the service, Becky and I walked back to the car, and as I sat down, overwhelmed with emotions, I started to sob, and the only words that came out were, "I believe." From that day on, things began to improve. I continued to pray, and I also continued to receive signs which usually came from a discussion with a friend. I began to learn that if I asked for guidance instead of making my own selfish plans, I would always hear the answers I needed to hear. Don't get me wrong; they weren't always the answers I wanted to hear, but the point is I started to listen.

Part of turning my life around also required me to continue to work on my health. By December of 2012, I was down 65 lbs and only had ten more to go before reaching my goal. I attended training sessions with Becky once a week, as well as boot camps throughout the summer. I started to surround myself with like-minded people, so I also learned the importance of accountability. Like I've mentioned before, we never have to take this journey alone, and having that additional support helped so much. That being said, I realize now that I had made one big mistake. Much like I had done in my addiction, I always went all in. I would develop tunnel vision along the way, which didn't allow for much flexibility. There was never much planning or thought about what if something went wrong. How would I adjust? What changes would I make? Nope screw all that, I was only focused on hitting my goal, and the rest didn't matter. The weight loss was also starting to get to my head. Pride was taking over, and I began to feel this false sense of confidence again. I was so close to achieving my goal, and people were noticing. Now you may ask, what's wrong with that? I should be proud of everything I've accomplished right! What I didn't realize back then that I do now, is that for someone who is always seeking validation from others to feel good about themselves, all the attention wasn't necessarily a good thing. I lacked humility, and I still hadn't learned to love myself yet. Even though I considered myself a good friend at the time, that dependence on others did not serve me well. I would need to learn how to stand on my own two feet if I was going to continue to grow. But of course, in the usual fashion, I had to learn everything the hard way.

**Lessons Learned:**

* I learned who my real friends were during this time. A few people who I thought would have supported my decision did not, but I knew I had to accept this, and instead, I opened the door to some new friendships.
* I learned that I couldn't change anyone. I could change myself and accept the results that came along with my actions. Sometimes those results aren't what we expect, but they just might be what we need.
* I saw that for things to change, everything has to change. A friend of mine told me once, "If nothing changes, nothing changes."
* To create the change I wanted to see in my life, I first had to admit I had a problem. Once that problem was apparent in my mind, I knew I would never want to go back there.
* Developing faith in a higher power has provided me guidance during times that I'm not always sure what to do. When I sit quietly and pray without selfish intentions and ask for guidance, I always hear what I need to here and so I can take action.

**Final Thoughts:**

Was there ever a time in your life where you lacked faith. Then by some devine intervention you finally came to believe there was something greater out there?

Share your story: info@theroadtohealth.me

**Suggested Solution:**

Sobriety takes work. I learned to accept my past, make my wrongs right, and then begin to change my actions and help others. If you feel as though you have a problem, you must first recognize it. Adding prayer to your day and provide guidance when you least expect it.

* See Tips & Resources

## SELF-DISCOVERY

Eight months after I decided to get sober, I felt as though everything in my life was falling into place. I had hit my weight loss goal, started to make new friendships, and I continued to do the work to have it all stay this way. What I didn't realize then and had been warned about was that the way I was focusing on my health wasn't sustainable. Much like in the past, I would go 100% all-in and obsess about the end goal until I either made it or I just got too exhausted to continue the journey. Although this time I had reached my goal, the effort it took to arrive there led me right into the world of complacency shortly after. I would work out six or seven days a week, eat nothing but chicken, broccoli, and rice, and then on the weekends, I splurged on the one treat meal I would allow myself to have. I even seem to remember being one month away from my goal and removing all foods that didn't fit the clean eating altogether, and as soon as I got there, I was going to celebrate. A friend of mine who had taken this journey with me also hit her goal, and so we decided it was time to go and enjoy a great meal together. Against our better judgment, we had both decided that we were going to relax for the entire weekend and not worry about eating as we usually did. After all, we deserved a break from all our hard work over the last year, and we assumed it would easy to pick back up on Monday. I had made the false assumption that this had now become a lifestyle for me, and there was no way I could mess it up.

The reality was that I had become obsessed and was exhausted from living this way. The positive side of this is that it would serve as one of the biggest lessons I would learn over the next few years when it came to my health. I had a great teacher that year and received excellent advice, but there was still that part of me that had to do things my own way. That meant going to the gym too often and not giving myself rest days, and I also didn't get very creative with what I ate, so it all became bland after a while. Today I have learned that sticking to something and creating a lifestyle takes some time, planning, and flexibility. It also means giving yourself grace and learning that you are not always going to make the right choices.

During the Spring of 2013, my debt has once again become unmanageable. Gary had given me the car, but it was a lot more than I could afford at the time. The brakes were starting to go, and I had no money to change them because all of our credit cards were maxed out. I was living paycheque to paycheque again, and the stress of not being able to manage my finances weighed heavily on me. Gary and I hadn't officially spoken about getting divorced yet, but we had become legally separated. He paid the mortgage and our line of credit while I had the vehicle as well as the credit cards. It finally got to a point where I felt I needed to file for bankruptcy. Because we were legally separated, I would be allowed to register on my own. I took on all the debt while Gary kept the condo so that he didn't have to foreclose. I would have to give up the vehicle, and so I had made arrangements with a friend from work to rent his car for the summer while I was waiting for Gary to pay me out for the condo. It was a very humbling experience for me. I remember coming home one day after work to find my car had been repossessed and was no longer in my driveway. I had officially lost it all, but for some strange reason, I felt as though I was given a fresh start at life.

During the summer, I also started to pick up some bad habits again. Because I wasn't as strict with my diet or my fitness, I decided that smoking was a good idea to start up again. After all, it would curb my hunger, and because I wasn't as diligent, this was a good thing. It happened gradually at first, but as with most addictions, it didn’t take long for it to become a full-blown habit again. I was experiencing a lot of stress at work, and I didn't manage my stress well at all, so I sought out means to achieve comfort outside of the healthy ways I had been taught over the last year. It was much easier for me to go outside and smoke a cigarette than it was to go and meditate for ten minutes. The reality was that I missed the feeling alcohol gave me, and so like I did with exercise the year before, smoking became one of my new ways to cope with stress. I also started to drink energy drinks daily, and fast food followed right behind that. There were times that I would pick up McDonald's on the way home, eat it in the car, stop off at a gas station to discard the evidence, and then go home and make myself some dinner. I didn't realize it back then, but I had only looked at addiction as being related to drugs and alcohol. I never saw food or other behaviors outside of that as a replacement for what I had used in the past. There is something called cross-addiction, where we give up one form of addiction and replace it with another. I had been doing this for years and never even realized it.

As time went on, I started to gain some of my weight back, not enough that it became a great concern to me, but it was happening slowly. It didn't help that I also started dating. I had gone a whole year without getting into a relationship, although I had gone on a couple of dates, which should have made me realize it was better to remain single a little longer, as usual, it did not. I wasn't always good at taking suggestions either when they were given to me. I had come along way over the last year, and I wanted to prove to the world that I had changed and could handle a relationship much better as a result of the work I had put in. Little did I know just because you stay single for a year does not mean you are equipped to be a good partner. I started dating this guy named Jack in early September, and in the usual fashion, I would overlook a lot of things that should have been red flags.

Jack worked evenings, so it only allowed us to see each other on the weekends. He would either come out to my place, and we would go out for dinner, or I would sometimes head out to his home when his roommate wasn't around. What I didn't see yet was that our relationship was starting with a bunch of lies. On our first date, he took me out for a nice dinner and ordered a glass of wine. I didn't think much of this because he already knew I didn't drink and mentioned he could take it or leave it several times during our conversations. Jack would also tell me he had a brother who had issues with addiction, so he fully understood what I was going through. Remember, when I said earlier, people who do not have a problem with alcohol don't feel the need to explain why or why not they drink? It all sounded very similar to what I would tell others. It should have served as red flag number one because every time we went out, he would feel the need to tell me he hadn't drank for a while and just had a stressful day. I am NOT trying to say he was an alcoholic or anything, but he still found the need to explain every time he drank. The second red flag came one evening when I went over to his place. Both of us were smokers, but yet this is something we failed to tell each other. I laugh today because this wasn't the first time I tried to be someone I'm not in the beginning stages of a relationship. I would always try and be who I thought they were looking for. The smoking only came out because while over at his place, he had a few glasses of wine. We had been hanging out most of the afternoon already, which was a long stretch to go without a cigarette. I finally looked over at Jack partway through the movie we were watching and confessed I smoked and needed to go out for one. I saw the look of relief on his face as he, too, admitted he did as well. We spent the rest of the evening outside walking, smoking, and laughing that neither one of us had the guts to tell the other.

Against my better judgment, I decided to move in with Jack a month or so later. I knew deep down that this wasn't a good idea, but I so badly wanted to be in a committed relationship again that I went against what I knew was right. Our relationship didn't last much longer after we moved in together. I learned that Jack drank a lot more than he claimed to drink because it's easy to hide when you don't live with someone. We never got to spend a lot of time together, so every once in a while, I would get up when he got home at 1 am to spend some time with him. We would watch TV for an hour, and I would go back to sleep because I had to wake up at 5 am. Every night after he got home, he would pour himself a glass of wine to relax, and that was usually followed up by another two or three drinks after that. It didn't concern me at first, but when we started to go out on the weekends with my friends or his family, more red flags started to come to light.

I remember going shopping for his daughter one day, and as we were making our way back to the car, I was telling him about our plans for the evening. We were going over to visit Bev and her husband that evening and thought it would be fun to have a games night. Jack stopped me all of a sudden and said, "I hope you don't think I'm not going to drink tonight!" I was a little surprised by his comment and how he said it, so I replied, "Of course not, I didn't say you couldn't!" He looked agitated for some strange reason. I had never really made mention of his drinking to that point, but I also realized that we had never really gone out yet on the weekend. What I would find out very shortly after was that when he drank with others on the weekend, he got out of hand very quickly. He was just trying to prepare me indirectly that this was going to happen. The following day was always filled with remorse and apologies. It was a behavior I was all too familiar with, and the more it happened, the more uncomfortable I got. We started fighting a lot after this, and I knew then that I had to cut this relationship short. It was a dangerous situation for me to be in, and I knew it. I had made arrangements the following day with a friend to go and stay with her and her husband for a few months, and so one evening while Jack was at work, I packed up all my shit and moved out. Jack wasn't a terrible guy, but for someone like myself, his drinking could eventually affect my own sobriety, and I was not about to give that up.

I spent the following summer enjoying myself and remained single. I dated a few times, but nothing serious came of it, and I was grateful for that. I ended up moving in with a good friend of mine for a year because the friends I was staying with loved to party, and sometimes that would involve coke. I didn't take this against them because they helped me get out of a bad situation. And regardless of their weekend activities, they were great people. I wasn't spending much time at the gym back then, and I was slowly letting myself go. Life was still pretty great, but because I wasn't keeping up on my physical health, my stress slowly started to increase. I was having trouble at work because I continued to take on more and more thinking it was the right thing to do. I was a people pleaser, and I felt as though the more work I took on, the better employee I was. I now realize that this behavior only hurt me in the end because I was overextended, couldn't say no, and started to build resentment towards my employer. I had been with the company for almost ten years, and the people there were like family to me. I hadn't yet learned to set boundaries in many areas of my life. My eagerness to please also started to affect some of my friendships because I would often make plans without realizing I already had a full plate and would end up canceling at the last minute. I was too tired and burnt out but wanted to make others happy. It never occurred to me that I could just say no to the invite and attempt to schedule some time at a later date when things weren't as busy. I would learn this valuable lesson a short time later when a fantastic friend of mine would call me out and set some distance between us because of my actions. I became known for canceling out at the last minute. Although my intentions were never to hurt anyone by it, I'm grateful I now had people in my life who didn't actually put up with it and taught me a valuable lesson instead. Today I plan everything much more carefully, and I'm happy to say I have developed the ability to say no when necessary.

I would learn a lot of lessons over the next five years, and even though I didn't see it back then, every mistake I made was a building block to finally start creating the life I wanted to live in the future. Up until that time, I was still trying to control everything in my life, and when things didn't work out, I would get frustrated and chalk it up to being someone else's fault or that I was a failure. This was very accurate with my current career as well. I didn't have the boundaries in place to say no when the workload became too much. I continued to put myself in a position where I would eventually harm someone else because of my actions. I was attempting to become more professional when, in fact, my frustration caused me to act the complete opposite, and this didn't help the company or me. I started to become a part of the problem rather than becoming part of the solution. After ten years, I decided it was time to try something new. I felt as though the company had changed too much and that I just didn't fit in anymore, when the reality was, yes the company had changed, but I just wasn't willing to provide any solutions anymore. I found out that the grass is not always greener on the other side. I had high hopes it would be, but even though it wasn't I am still glad I went to go find out myself instead of taking someone else word for it.

It was time for a fresh start. I had a lot of good things going on in my life, so I wanted to continue that trend. I was in a relationship again and learning how to be a better partner. I also wanted to use this new career opportunity to learn how to be a better coworker and leader. So needless to stay, I jumped into my new job with a lot of excitement and enthusiasm. After getting the rundown of what the job entailed, I knew I had a lot of experience and value to bring to the table. This was the first time in a very long time that I started to feel some self-worth. Unfortunately, there was still one thing that stood in the way of genuinely discovering who I was meant to be, and that was my people-pleasing habit. Like with everything else I took on in life, I wanted to do my best, and this was no different. The problem was that I was always doing my best to show others my value, and when I felt they didn't see it, I got discouraged and thought there was something wrong with me. The searching for recognition that had haunted me since I was a child was starting to rear its ugly head again. The crazy part is that over the first few months of my employment, I would often be told by my boss about what a fantastic job I was doing, but yet it was as though my mind was blocking that out and telling me I could do better. I started to become obsessed with taking on more and more until eventually, I landed myself in a position where it became too much.

The stress from work would eventually start to take a toll on my health. No matter how hard I tried to swear off energy drinks, smoking, and fast food, they would always sneak back in over time, and I started to beat myself up about it. I was gaining back the weight that I promised myself I would keep off, and every new diet I tried was just another attempt at a quick fix solution. It had taken me a full year to lose 75 pounds, and it also took a lot of work. I had now gained back about 40 pounds, and my self-esteem was starting to suffer as a result. I tried different types of cleanses, diet supplements, and even low carb plans, though I had no idea what I was doing. For some reason, I was no longer interested in putting the time in and doing the actual work it took to be successful. The desire to lose weight, coupled with the need to be recognized in my work life, didn't make for a good combination. I started picking up some old behaviors I had worked so hard to let go of. If there were ever a time in my sobriety that could have sent me over the edge, it was this time. Although I hadn't entirely stopped doing the work altogether, I was stuck in a world of complacency. I was worn out and doing nothing to improve my situation. This can be a slippery slope for someone with my history, so I knew it would only be a matter of time before things fell apart if I wasn't careful. All of these events, however, would eventually be the inspiration I needed to change my mindset and improve my life.

**Lessons Learned:**

* After I lost everything I felt as though a weight had been lifted off my shoulders. I didn't need "stuff" to experience happiness, I needed less.
* It takes much more energy to have a bad day rather than a good day.
* The mistakes I've made in life or what I've perceived as failures would become my greatest assets and teaching

tools.

**Final Thoughts:**

**Suggested Solution:**

Take a look at the story you are currently telling yourself. Do you have roadblocks that always get in the way? Do you see patterns that continue to appear in your life and de-rail you? When we recognize the things that block us and create solutions for them, we can often start morning forward. Take some time and re-write your story to how you want to live and bring yourself closer to that.

## MINDSET SHIFT

First off, I want to start by saying that I don't feel as though determination was something that came naturally to me; it was something I had to work hard at developing. Before I developed commitment and passion, I was stuck in the world of procrastination. I was the master of starting something and never carrying it out. It's something that drives me even more in my life now. My passion for what I do today came from discovering my purpose in life. I used to look at my past as one big failure with an abundance of different screw-up moments. Today I use these stories and mistakes to fuel my passion for serving others by sharing my experience and how I moved through the pain and hopelessness. My passion now moves me forward.

In early 2019 I needed a little bit of inspiration, and so I went to the person I knew could help. I called up Bev and asked her if we could get together for a visit. If there was one person who had been my rock through this entire journey, it was her, and anytime I went to Bev for advice, I always felt better afterward. So this time was no different, and I told her what was going on and that I needed a little motivation in my life because I felt like I was going backward again. She mentioned that recently she started to listen to podcasts and had a few to recommend. I honestly had never heard of a podcast before, so I wasn't all that sure what they were. I noted some down and made a promise to myself that I would start to listen to at least one a day. I started up with some motivational podcasts, which I enjoyed. It felt as though I was getting a free education, which mostly I was.

About a month later, I decided I was going to head down to California to celebrate my birthday with Kathy and her husband. Kathy and I had always talked about health and fitness together because we had both struggled in this area. When we got together, we usually ended up indulging in things that were entirely not health-related, but I will own that fact that we enjoyed every minute of it. We would always try and balance out our meals for the day and share new ideas we had both been trying out. I think this was the first time I started to become a little bit more open-minded around the topic of health and nutrition. Kathy would always try new things out to see if they worked or not. I felt as though because I had lost a lot of weight back when I got sober that THAT was the only way it could be done. I became opinionated about anything else that didn't fit into the mold I had used in the past. I also came to find out during that visit that Kathy also listened to podcasts often and recommended a few around fitness. Once again, this encouraged me to add to my list of shows.

When I got home after that weekend, I started to do some research. I would look at all the podcasts that were in the health and fitness categories and start listening to them one by one until I finally found one that started to resonate with me. Much like when I got sober, part of my success was finding people who could relate to what I had gone through. I then started to surround myself with those people who had what I wanted in life and do what they did. I got in the car one morning to go to work and started to scroll through the list of shows that I had saved. I came across one called The Million Pound Mission, by Adam Schaeuble. I randomly picked an episode and started to make my way to work. Ok, first off, Adam had a fantastic voice, so this drew me in from the start. Second, after listening for a few minutes, I felt as though he was talking to me. It was an episode where he does a deep dive with one of his clients. I could relate to what his client was going through. Up until this point, I had always read about health and nutrition coming from the viewpoint of the experts. I had never actually heard both sides of the story before. As his client explained the current struggles they were experiencing at the time, Adam would draw as much information as he could out of the client and then start to provide some solutions that were entirely directed to the needs of his clients. I was used to hearing the same advice being recommended by experts as though health was a one size fits all plan so this was new. It was very tailored advice based on what the individual's goals were. The more I listened, the more I heard that a lot of his clients were on different types of meal plans. Some were Keto Based while others were Paleo or Whole Food-based. At the end of each episode, Adam mentioned a group he facilitated to help people reach their goals. He was dedicated to assisting people in losing a total of one million pounds. The more I listened, the more I wanted to become a part of this movement, so one afternoon when I got home from work, I decided to visit his website. I emailed Adam to ask him a few questions before I got started, and to my surprise, he emailed back the next day. I was impressed that I got a response so quickly, so I decided to sign up right away.

I found that after joining Adam's group, I was injected with a new sense of purpose. I enjoyed partaking in the group discussions, the live video chats, and of course our one on one coaching calls with Adam himself. It was the first time I had been a part of an online community like this one, and I loved it. The community members became like a second family for me because we all held each other accountable. I was starting to feel as though things were moving in the right direction again. I felt as though my willpower was beginning to increase as opposed to feeling like I had none at all. I even booked a session with my amazing massage therapist one afternoon for some self-care, and she mentioned she could notice the excitement in my voice. It was as though a switch had flipped inside of me, and I could suddenly see a clear vision of the future I wanted to create for myself.

By the spring of 2019, I started to develop a new routine and adopt some new habits. Even though the stress at work hadn't gone away, I knew that if I didn't start to take care of my health, everything else would begin to fall apart. One of the areas I was having trouble staying consistent in was my workouts. I wanted to go workout, but if I left them for the afternoon, I would always find some sort of justification or excuse as to why I couldn't go. So one of the first things I changed was the time I went. I had gone first thing in the morning before, and in all honesty, I never enjoyed it much back then. This time around, I also started work a lot earlier, and so if I was going to make the switch, I would have to wake up much earlier than I had in the past. So I started slowly. I would wake up 30 minutes earlier so I could fully enjoy a cup of coffee before getting ready for work. When that started to become regular, I woke up an hour earlier and went for a quick 30-minute workout. I kept things short and manageable at first because, as history told me, anytime I took on too much without a plan and doing too much all at once, I would fall short. I needed time to adjust and create the right mindset to gain momentum. Once I developed a new habit, it took much less will power than it did to begin with, and I could continue to add. This way of doing things also allowed me to gain confidence in my own ability to achieve my goals.

A few months later, I was waking up every morning around 4 am to hit the gym four days a week, and most of the time, I would even wake up before my alarm because my body adapted to this new schedule. I started going to bed earlier, which took some time to adjust to, but with the stress from work, I was mentally exhausted by the end of the day anyway.

Right around the same time, I started to have sharp chest pains and shortness of breath. I had been an off and on smoker for years, and after I quit smoking, I took on vaping. I had given up vaping in December the year earlier, so when I first started having the shortness of breath, I didn't think much of it and thought it would go away eventually. Well, it did not, and along with that came the chest pains, which started to concern me a little. They would happen at random times of the day, so I couldn't figure out what was causing them. When they started to happen more frequently, I finally made an appointment with my doctor. The day before the appointment, I was sitting at work when all of a sudden, the chest pains got more serious, and my left arm started to go completely numb. As I was shaking my arm, one of my co-workers took notice and asked what was wrong. I told her about the pain in my chest and the numbness of my arm, and she jumped out of her chair and told me she was taking me to the hospital. Her spouse had heart conditions, so she was familiar with the signs of possible heart issues. I got my jacket on and made my way to the car. As we drove to the hospital, and my friend talked about the possibility of what could be going wrong, all I could think of was that I was too young to be having heart problems. That being said, I had put my body through so much strain over the last twenty years. I guess it shouldn't have come as a surprise. When we arrived at the hospital, I went to go check-in. When they asked me what I was in for, I explained the situation. This would be the first time I'd been to a hospital where I didn't have to wait for hours to see a doctor. They brought me right in right away and started doing tests to determine if I was, in fact, having a heart attack. I'm not going to lie; although I managed to stay fairly positive thought the experience, I was scared shitless. They had to keep me at the hospital for another six hours before they could run a second set of tests, so I had a lot of time to think about why this was happening and the changes I would be making moving forward. About an hour after my last set of tests, the doctor came in to see me. The first question he asked was if I was under a lot of stress currently. I was used to stress by now, so I told him, "A little maybe, why? Do you think it's stress-related?" He explained that it could be several things, and to be safe; he was going to get me in for a stress test to be sure. He did, however, rule out a heart attack, so that made me feel a lot better. I was told to take a few days off of work to see if the chest pain would subside a little, and it did.

A few weeks later, I went back into the hospital to perform a stress test. I was grateful I had been going to the gym regularly because it was not easy walking on a sharp incline at a swift pace. After the test had been completed, I sat down with the cardiologist. She asked me if I was a regular at the gym, to which I responded yes. She then proceeded to tell me that my heart was really strong, and in that instant, a feeling of relief washed over me. The doctor, however, looked at me with care and concern and asked, "How much stress are you under right now?" The previous doctor had asked me the same thing, and so I gave the same response. She then went on to explain that if it was stress that I was experiencing, then I had to start managing it better. She went over a list of all the side effects stress caused and explained that if I didn't learn to alleviate it, I might end up back here with more severe consequences. I went home that day and decided that it was time to start expanding my list of good habits.

The first habit I put in place was to stop drinking energy drinks. I replaced them with one cup of coffee in the morning, and that was it. I also started to look for a new job as my current one just wasn't a good fit anymore. In the process of asking my old boss for a reference, he ended up asking me out for lunch instead. He mentioned that he had a position in outside sales open and that if I were interested, they would love to have me back. We had a great chat about how things were when I left the company a couple of years prior and also the value I would provide by returning. I had the advantage of already having a good relationship with the customers I would be seeing, and in all honesty, the people I had worked with had always felt like family. When I went in after work for my first official interview, I was met with some familiar faces and a lot of hugs. It pretty much solidified the deal, and a few weeks later, my current company and I parted ways. I was excited and also nervous about being in outside sales and traveling for a living. I had traveled for work before, but this was all new because now I was going to be doing it much more frequently. In the past, when I had traveled for business, I would often use it as an excuse to try all the local cuisines and not exactly eat all that healthy. I had trouble sleeping in hotels as well, so health started to become a bit of a concern. If this was going to be a part of my daily life, I had to come up with a plan so that I didn't let up on the good habits I had developed over the last seven months.

The first thing I did was book a one on one coaching call

with Adam. I knew that if I was going to continue to carry on the momentum I had built up, I had to start adding some additional strategies to my list. It was then that Adam taught me about calorie and carb cycling. I was already tracking my food daily, so now I could use these additional tools to manage my daily calories on the road according to my plans. On days where I had a light load and was doing mostly computer work, I could use a low-calorie day, and on days I had a client lunch or not as many options food-wise, I could plan a higher day. I also sought out gym locations around where I was staying because the hotel gyms didn't always have the equipment I enjoyed using. I found hotels close to those gyms, and because I had a membership to the sister gyms up in Canada, I could use the US gyms for no additional cost. I was excited for the first time in a long time because I felt as though with the help of Adam and his community, I could make this all work. I had made some new friends in the group as well, so the support and accountability I had when I started my new job kept me on track and feeling good. There were a lot of temptations on the road when I first started, so having a plan, being more flexible, and managing my days according to the plan I had created made things less stressful and overwhelming. I joined all our community group chats when on the road, so it kept me feeling connected. During one of our chats, Adam announced that he was having an event down in Huntington Beach,

California. It was only a two-hour flight for me and relatively inexpensive, so I reached out to one of my friends, Paula, in the group that mentioned she might also want to go. We decided to room together to cut down the cost of the trip, and Paula graciously offered to pick me up from the airport as well. Little did I know it at the time, but this would be a life-changing weekend I would never forget.

**Lessons Learned:**

* I had to be more open-minded when it came to my health. I had been very opinionated of what was right and wrong instead of what was right for me. I found that what was right for me may not be right for someone else. There is more than one way to accomplish your goals!
* I accepted that this journey was better when surrounded by the support of others that were on the same path as I was. I have learned so many things from the communities I have been a part of.
* Even though I still have bad days here and there, the emotions I experienced during those times aren't as high and low. They are a little more steady.
* Reaching out for help did not make me weak; It meant that I was willing to become more vulnerable, which turned into my strength.

**Final Thoughts:**

* Have you found yourself stuck in the same cycles over and over when it comes to your health? Do you want to break free of these and change your mindset?

I'd love to hear your story. Info@theroadtohealth.me

**Suggested Solution:**

Learning to create more time in my day has helped me become more productive. Below is a course that may help! Or you can write out a list of things you do daily and start to prioritize them.

* Time God & Goddess Revolution
www.marisaimon.com/timegodrevolution

Get support and accountability in your life. You don't have to take this journey alone. Join our Facebook Group! - The Road to Health Podcast

## ELEVATED

On Thursday, September 19th, I arrived at Los Angeles International airport. I texted Paula to let her know my flight had landed, and she responded, letting me know she was stuck in traffic but was only a short distance away and would be there soon. I was super excited, and although I had never met Paula in person before, somehow I just knew we would hit it off. I mean, someone who is willing to pick you up from LAX at 5 pm during LA rush hour has to be an incredibly kind person. When Paula pulled up, and we greeted each other with a big hug, I felt as though I was meeting up with an old friend. We had plenty of time to get acquainted because of the traffic and the time it took for us to arrive at the hotel. After we arrived, we checked in and decided to grab something to eat. We were both super excited for the event that Saturday, and Adam had also suggested we get together on Friday for a visit so needless to say the energy was very high. We had a hard time getting to sleep that first night because of how much we had to talk about, but as we were both on a similar schedule, we made sure to shut it down at a reasonable hour. Paula has become a very close friend of mine today, and if there is one thing you should know about us, we are incredibly high energy when put in the same room.

The next morning, Paula and I went down to the lobby for breakfast and planned out our day. We headed down to the beach for a couple of hours, walked around, did a little shopping and sightseeing. After that, we went for an early lunch and got a message to meet up with Adam over in West Hollywood, where he was staying with a friend. That friend happened to be Allison Melody from Food Heals, and so now we were even more excited because we would get the chance to meet another one of our favorite podcasters. She also happened to be one of the keynote speakers at Adam's event on Saturday. When we arrived, Adam and Allison came out to greet us. It felt a little surreal, to be honest, because hearing someone on a podcast weekly and then actually meeting them in person was kind of cool. Plus, both Adam and Allison had so much passion for their missions that it was hard not to feel positive and excited around them. Adam took us out for lunch, and we got to catch up and hear about the plan for Saturday as well as some new ideas he had for the community we were a part of. After lunch, we went back to Allison's place and spent some time in her studio recording some live casts and just shooting the shit. Shortly before dinner, Paula and I stopped off at the Santa Monica Pier for a quick visit and then headed back to the hotel. We grabbed a bite to eat and went up to the room to recap our day. We were overwhelmed with excitement from our day, and since we were able to hang out with two people we respected in the podcasting world, it made it even better. We started to discuss the potential of starting up our own podcasts and the ideas we had. Paula pointed out that with me always traveling, I could start a podcast on how to get healthy while traveling for business. I thought this was a great idea because not only would this hold me accountable, but maybe I could inspire others to start their journey alongside me.

Saturday morning Paula and I both woke up super excited. We had a relaxing morning and just shared our ideas of what we had hoped to get out of the event that day. While grabbing some lunch, Adam texted us and mentioned we could head over early to meet some of the other speakers before everyone else arrived. When we got there, Adam introduced us to all the speakers, and we had a chance to chat with everyone. I would also meet my friend Kris McPeak from the Elevate Your 8 Podcast, who would eventually become my entrepreneurial partner in crime, but unfortunately, during this visit, Kris and I never really had a chance to chat.

As the speakers went up to share their stories, I was in awe of how real and vulnerable they were. You could tell by the way they spoke that they were all incredibly passionate about what they stood for and clear about their vision. Even though the event was only half a day, I felt as though

I had gotten a full weekend's worth of information. I don't think I've ever been that fired up before, and to top it all off after the event was over, Adam invited us to go out for dinner with the rest of the speakers. Even though Paula and I had planned on going back to the hotel and talking about everything that had transpired over the weekend, it was hard to pass up an invite like this. As we ate, we got to hear about what life was like to be a podcaster and entrepreneur. At one point during the evening, Allison and I were having a conversation about my idea to start a podcast. If you know Allison at all or have listened to her show Food Heals, you know that she is super passionate about what she does. Until this point in my life, I had been quiet about sharing my whole story other than to those that were close to me. She told me that evening that if I had a story to share, and it could help others that it was my responsibility to share it. This statement moved me because although I had been helping others to learn how to stay sober, I had never really extended my reach past the world of recovery. I hadn't looked at my past experiences as an asset; rather, as a series of screw-ups. Until I started to write this book, I didn't see just how valuable all of those experiences were. Even a university education wouldn't cover the knowledge I gained from living it myself.

After I had gotten home from Los Angeles, I was inspired

more than I ever had been before. I made some fantastic friendships that weekend, and now I had a clearer vision of who I wanted to be. I got on a call with Adam right away and told him about the idea I had for starting my podcast. He loved it, and we got to work right away, putting together all the details. Adam loved the idea of sharing my journey to get healthy in a real and honest way while traveling for business. This is where The Road to Health Podcast was born. Over the next few months, I purchased the equipment I required, joined various communities to learn what I needed to know, and also signed up for a few courses that would help me get started. In October, Allison had mentioned she had a mastermind group called Rise & Bloom, which helped entrepreneurs create impact and influence doing what you love. Being as I now had a clearer vision of what I wanted to do in life, I felt as though this mastermind would help me grow even more.

On December 16th, 2019, I launched the first episode of The Road to Health Podcast. I was so nervous in the beginning because I struggled with the limiting belief that no one would take me seriously. So my goal became to be as honest and vulnerable as possible with what I shared. This meant that not only was I going to share my goals I was accomplishing throughout my journey, but also the struggles as well. I could never relate to people who hadn't had some sort of conflict to get to where they were. When I got sober, it was essential to speak with others who had experienced the same thing. I looked at this new journey as a way to inspire hope and allow others to be able to relate. The reality is that life is never going to be perfect; we all face struggles sometimes. In my own experience, learning how to move through those hard times and create solutions with the help of others has allowed me to become the person I am today. I am not afraid to ask for help or admit when I'm wrong, which is something I was never able to do before. I also realize that this is a journey we never have to take alone. By increasing my circle and surrounding myself with other likeminded people, it has increased my confidence in my ability to do things I never thought were possible. I finally felt as though I was heading in the right direction and now had my own mission.

In early 2020, I started to notice the efforts of my weight loss journey. Being accountable through my show was helping me stay open-minded about learning as much as I could to make my road even better. My spouse and I went to Mexico for a vacation in early February. While I was there, I listened to a podcast that a doctor was featured on. The show was about how carbs could be included in the same category as drugs and alcohol because of how addictive they could be for some people. This statement piqued my curiosity because this was a subject that I could now relate too. The next thing I heard would change the way I looked at particular foods. The doctor stated, would you give an alcoholic two beers a day, tell them to maintain that amount and use their will power to do so? I couldn't even imagine only having two drinks per day and being told I could have no more, but the reality is that was what I had been doing when it came to my diet! Two beers would eventually, over time, lead to some table dancing and good old blackouts, and that wasn't good for anyone involved. I did the same thing with food, minus the blackouts, of course. I laughed because just that morning I had been standing in line waiting for my omelet at the buffet when I grabbed two pastries and ate them while I waited so that my spouse didn't see I had eaten them. The reality was that I was on vacation, and I shouldn't have been ashamed to eat something I enjoyed in the first place! Why the hell was I hiding it? Although I knew that sugar affected me in this way, this is the first time I can remember looking at it as an addiction. Even though I wasn't crazy about the idea of eliminating sugar altogether, I felt inspired to give it a try and see what the outcome would be. I'm grateful I had learned to be more open-minded.

After we returned home, I signed up for a program called Deeper State Keto. I was already tracking my food, and this would just mean that I would start tracking my macros as well. I wasn't crazy about doing a low carb diet again, but I was determined to hit my goal in June, and I was willing to try it out and see if it was indeed something that worked for my body. I had always looked at a diet as restrictive and challenging, and while working with Adam over the last few months, I came to believe that it didn't have to be that way. Everything I was already doing was working except I had one crutch left, and that was sugar. I traveled for the next five out of seven weeks and was diligent about tracking my food. The first couple of weeks were the hardest, but after that point, I had started to become creative enough in my food selection that it became more comfortable, and I didn't feel as though I was depriving myself. I enjoyed what I ate, and as a result, it took minimal effort on my part other than having to track everything. I was very fortunate that I also had friends who were doing the program, so this made it even better because we could share our experiences around it. Accountability had become a key component for me.

While I was working on my health, I was also starting to get more involved with creating my own business. I loved what I did during the day, but I felt as though I could also make a difference by coaching others on evenings and weekends. I wanted to make a difference, and because of all the amazing people I now had in my circle, I felt as though it was possible. I took a course in life coaching and also started to get more involved in Allison's Rise & Bloom mastermind. I felt as though the support I received from the group was elevating me to another level. The friendships I had established kept me moving forward even when I had doubts along the way. I learned how to create my website, course, landing pages, and so much more. I finally started to feel as though I had a purpose in life.

In March of 2020, our world was hit with a virus that changed the way we lived and functioned on a day to day basis. I had been traveling a lot before this, and all of a sudden, I found myself stuck working from home. Even though I had experience working from home in between trips, staying put for so long wasn't a super easy change to make. The benefit I had was that I had been experimenting with so many different things in terms of my health that I felt as though I had the means to deal with this very unreal situation we all faced. I had changed my gym workouts to resistant band training that I did in my hotel room, so the gym's closing didn't affect me all that much. It just meant I didn't have to wake up as early to get in my workouts. I also kept to my low carb program, and now I could more easily control my food intake because I was making it myself. Even though we had never been through something like this before, my typical response to a roadblock would often lead to complacency. This was the last thing I wanted to have happen again, and because of my newfound purpose in life, I took this as an opportunity to really dig in and work even harder. I started waking up even earlier so that I had the additional time in the morning to be creative and work on my business. Then after work, I would spend time online in video chats getting the support I needed from friends and the education to do even more. Although there were undoubtedly times I came close to burning myself out; I had also learned that it was essential to take a break once in a while. I started to get organized and prioritize what I did in a day. Much as with my addiction to substances, I knew that I could also get too carried away with filling my time trying to build my business.

Today even though I know I will stumble and face challenges in my life, I stand tall and proud of my accomplishments. I now understand that the journey I am on will be imperfect at times and might get ugly, but I am where I'm meant to be at this very moment because of what I've been through. I don't look at a life of drug and alcohol addiction as something negative because my experience can now help others going through the same things. The support I have received from family and friends has filled me with so much joy and love. I've also found a way to love myself again, and although I still struggle with life some days, I've learned to develop a healthy mindset, which helps me deal with what life throws at me a little easier than before. This new mindset has allowed me to continue on a path of personal growth and has empowered me to develop the firm belief in my ability to make my dreams come true. I hope that through sharing my story, it inspires you to make the positive changes you seek in your own life and to never give up on living the life of your dreams.

**Lesson Learned:**

* Waking up early in the morning has given me the time to do what I need to get done for myself. I have found that I am at my best in the hours when no one else is awake. I'm in flow!
* Recognizing roadblocks that have stopped me from reaching my goals in the past, has allowed me to create solutions to move past them.
* Creating small habits over time has allowed me to take many steps forward in the right direction, and before I knew it, I hit my first goal.
* Surrounding myself with people who have a similar purpose in life fuels my passion even more than I thought possible. A strong inner circle has changed so many aspects of my life.
* I have learned that doing what I love, which is helping others gain the belief in their ability to change, it has led to a more fulfilling life.

* When I work on removing my limiting beliefs, I open the door to what would have been a missed opportunity. My dreams start to become a reality. (This book if proof of that!)
* Do something you love and are passionate about!
* By accepting my past, I have gained the clarity I needed to develop a healthy mindset.

**Final Thoughts:**

My life has changed due to the fact I have now realized I'm worth the effort I put in. I have developed a routine that allows me more flexibility and time. By prioritizing my own needs first, I've been able to achieve things I never thought were possible. Believe it or not, I actually enjoy going to bed early so that I can wake up and do what I love in the morning. Here is what an average day looks like for me:

Wake up: 4:30am
* Meditation
* Workout
* Make a delicious frothy Keto Coffee
* Read my affirmations
* Get creative by working on my podcast, writing, or anything to grow my side hustle.
* Get ready for work or if a weekend I continue to create!

7am - 4pm - Work
* Visiting Clients or Working from Home/Office
* Get a meditation session in during the day.
* Go for a 30-minute walk if I have time.

4pm - 6pm
* Have something to eat.
* Attend a mastermind, learning something new, or create more content. This is education time for me.

6pm - 8pm
* Wind down by reading a book.
* Spend some time watching a Netflix show with my spouse or time with friends.
* Some more reading before I fall asleep.
* Meditation before bed.

I never thought I could make getting up so early work for me until I committed to the change. Today it's become a routine I love so that I can help others do the same!

**Suggested Solution:**

I have used many different resources to achieve my goals today. I have added a resources page at the back of this book with a bonus content link just for you!

* See Tips & Resources (Don't miss out on the bonus content page!)

## AFTERWORD

Writing this book was an emotional rollercoaster of digging up the past and re-living so many things that I have long since hidden away. I'm honored to share this journey with you and grateful you choose to be a part of it. The purpose of this book is to help others accept their past, gain clarity, and learn to develop a healthy mindset. It serves as a reminder that no matter what struggles we've been through, we all have the ability to overcome them. The mistakes I've made have served as lessons that now fuel my passion for helping others. I've carried the shame from my past for too long. This book was a means to release that shame once and for all. I hope that by being open and vulnerable, it can also help others to do the same. By sharing my story, I have found a lot of peace and healing. Even though I wasn't proud of who I was back, then I remind myself that it's not who I am today. I am proud of the fact that I have been able to use what I'd learned to develop a better future and help mentor others as a result.

I'm here today because of the people that have walked this journey beside me. I never once had to go at it alone. These people never gave up on me and gave me the strength to believe in myself again. I am full of love and joy as a result and couldn't be more grateful for the life I live today.

Keep moving forward and never give up!

With Love,
Tamar Medford

## TIPS & RESOURCES

**Website:** www.theroadforward.ca

Bonus Offer for Readers!
Wake Up on Fire Workshop (FREE) www.theroadforward.ca

**Coaching Services/Programs/Courses:**

Tamar offers performance consulting to individuals, groups and corporate teams. To learn more, visit her website or email below.

General Inquiries: info@theroadtohealth.me
Website: www.theroadforward.ca

**Social Media Links:**

Instagram: @theroadtoheathpc
Facebook: The Road Forward
Twitter: @roadtohealthpc
Pinterest: Roadtohealthpodcast

**Other Resources:**

Adam gave me so many new health and fitness tools, as well as taught me how to start my podcast!
Adam Schaeuble: Free Mission Possible Community - www.transformationcoach.me
Podcast: The Million Pound Mission Podcast
Podcast: Casting the Pod

Allison has taught me most of what I know when it comes to my entrepreneurial and social media skills.
Allison Melody: Food Heals & Rise & Bloom Mastermind
www.foodhealsnation.com
Podcast: Food Heals Podcast

Marisa taught me how to meditate like a boss!
Marisa Imon - www.marisaimon.com
Podcast: Incandescent Podcast
Meditations: www.marisaimon.com/freemeditations

Kris will teach you how to increase your productivity in the 8 hours a day you are not working or sleeping!
Kris McPeak
www.krismcpeak.com
Podcast: The Elevate Your 8 Podcast

Kelsey will give you the tools you need to live a super fun and positive life!
Kelsey Henry: Positively Delighted

www.positivelydelighted.com
Podcast: The Positively Delighted Show

**Here is a list of my favourite apps to keep me organized and on track!**

Habit Tracker:
Streaks
Strides

Food Tracking:
MyFitnessPal
Carb Manager

Workouts:
Map My Fitness Under Armour

Meditation:
Calm
Headspace

Journal/Gratitude:
Five Minute Journal
Day One

Keep Organized!
OneNote

Google Keep

**Some Of My Favourite Podcasts!**

The Road to Health - Tamar Medford (Hey that's me!)
The Million Pound Mission - Adam Schaeuble
Achieve Your Goals with Hal Elrod
Aww Shift - Anthony Trucks
The Elevate Your 8 Podcast - Kris McPeak
Do A Day with Bryan Falchuk
Food Heals - Allison Melody
Incandescent - Marisa Imon (Use for Meditation!)
Let's Veg About It Podcast - Annette White
Lost AF Wellness - Paula Miller
The Keto Savage Podcast - Robert Sikes
The Positively Delighted Show - Kelsey Henry
The Model Health Show - Shawn Stevenson
Smart Passive Income - Pat Flynn
The Toxin Terminator - Aimee Carlson
Powers Hour - Laura Powers
Beauty Call Podcast - Janice McQueen

## ABOUT THE AUTHOR

Tamar has a career in sales, is a professional life coach, podcast host, and champion to people who suffer from addiction. After living through 20 years of addiction herself, she finally decided to turn her life around and embarked on a mission to inspire others to do the same. Her passion lies in helping people break free of their unhealthy and addictive patterns. She empowers people to live up to their true potential and meet the challenge of change. When she's not traveling for business, she enjoys creating new content for her show, The Road to Health, and spending time with family and friends. Starting the show has inspired her to continue on this journey of self-improvement. By learning how to achieve her own goals more effectively and by developing a healthier mindset, she can now help coach others to do the same.

You can find more information about Tamar, her podcast and coaching services at www.theroadforward.ca

Made in USA - Kendallville, IN
1237169_9781777255602
02.22.2021 0909